BE YOUR OWN BRAND OF SEXY

A New Sexual Revolution for Women

Susan L. Edelman, MD

OPTIONS PRESS

PALO ALTO, CALIFORNIA

Copyright © 2015 by Susan L. Edelman, MD.

All rights reserved. No part of this book may be reproduced or transmitted in any form or by any means, electronic or mechanical, including photocopying, recording, or by any information storage and retrieval system without written permission from the publisher, except for the inclusion of brief quotations in a review.

Options Press
P.O. Box 150
Palo Alto, CA 94302
www.beyourownbrandofsexy.com
www.optionspress.com
info@optionspress.com

ISBN 10: 1-942-34322-1
ISBN 13: 978-1-942343-22-6

First edition 2015

Cover design: Kimberly A. Soderstrom
Interior design: Blue Iris Design

Library of Congress Control Number: 2014922361

Botox, Hush Puppies, Photoshop, Spanx, Viagra, and Vicodin are registered trademarks.

Be Your Own Brand of Sexy is a trademark of Susan L. Edelman, MD.

Options Press and Options Press logo are both trademarks of Options Press Corporation.

10 9 8 7 6 5 4 3 2 1

Printed in the United States of America.

This is an important book. It reveals sociology and psychological insights for young women to explore who they are and make romantic decisions wisely. Additionally, Dr. Edelman's call for a return to sisterhood is compelling. Women will learn much from her wisdom.

—*Mali Mann, MD, Training and Supervising Psychoanalyst, San Francisco Center for Psychoanalysis, Adjunct Clinical Professor, Department of Psychiatry and Behavioral Sciences, Stanford University Medical*

Navigating the gender divide has become increasingly complicated following the feminist revolution. In *Be Your Own Brand of Sexy*, Dr. Edelman shows the reader how to craft a relationship solution that fits their own personal needs without sacrificing important standards. I believe *Be Your Own Brand of Sexy* will soon become a much-needed classic.

—*Hans Steiner, MD, Professor Emeritus (Active), Psychiatry and Human Development, Stanford University, School of Medicine*

To my parents,
who foolishly told me I could
accomplish anything.

To my patients,
who taught me what I needed
to know to write this book.

And to Emma,
who wanted me to change the world.

Thank you!

Contents

- Confidence Is Sexy—Self-Knowledge Is Power
- Moving Forward

Board-certified psychiatrist Dr. Susan Edelman has spent 29 years as a practicing therapist in Palo Alto, California, specializing in women's issues. As a single woman, she's been on the front lines of dating. Living in Louisiana and then California gave her two very different perspectives on dating, helping her see all the options women have. She enjoys dancing, gardening, and traveling. Perhaps you will see some of her interests reflected in this book.

In addition to her private practice, Dr. Edelman is an Adjunct Clinical Associate Professor at Stanford University in the Department of Psychiatry and Behavioral Sciences. Dr. Edelman received her undergraduate and medical degrees from Louisiana State University. She completed her psychiatric residency at Tulane University School of Medicine.

Preface

Over the 29 years I've been in private practice, I've realized that, despite the advances we've made, women across generations still struggle with having a voice and standing up for themselves. We think it's getting better, but it's not.

That same struggle is why they don't get what they want from men. It's painful, and in many cases it stops them from getting what they want out of life.

My wonderful patients deserve better—and this is not just a problem for them. It's global, and we need a new revolution to create change.

That's why I wrote this book. I want to support the women who will never walk through my office door yet need a helping hand.

Although this book was written for single women about sexuality and relationships, the principles are universal. One reader told me these chapters helped her with a problem at work. Male readers say that, thanks to the ideas in this book, they are better able to ask for what they want and improve their relationships. It has helped mothers to become better informed and understand how to guide their children.

Be yourself. The message of this book is not new, but it is timeless. Being yourself can be difficult to accomplish when outside forces pull us in different directions. People advise, criticize, compete, and reject us. Media shows us what everyone else appears to be doing. Staying on our paths can be challenging but worth the effort.

This book may only be the tip of the iceberg of exploration for some of you. I've tried to make the stories here common and relatable to many people, but a self-help book cannot replace a consultation with an expert. Please find a psychiatrist or therapist if you're still struggling after reading this book. I'll have information about how to find experts on my website, www.beyourownbrandofsexy.com.

I hope to entertain, educate, and tweak your perspective on your life and the world that influences your decisions. Embracing our similarities rather than our differences can bring us closer together.

If you want to read more on these subjects, Appendix A gives a list of related materials. If you have questions or suggestions, contact me at: info@beyourownbrandofsexy.com.

Acknowledgements

When I first told people I was writing a book about sex, I was surprised to discover that not everyone was supportive. Maybe I was naïve. Then a wise man told me that I should be pleased with the firestorm of controversy that my ideas were causing. That without it, my message wouldn't travel to change the world. That gave me a sense of internal peace that I hope will last after my book is published. Writing a book about individuality requires gathering a lot of different opinions. I'm grateful to those who cared enough to share their views and ideas with me, even when they differed from my own.

Acceptance of my book project was vital to my morale, so I am grateful for the encouragement I received from the local psychiatric community, especially Drs. John Barry and Mary Ann Norfleet. I feel fortunate for the support and friendship of Drs. Rosaline Vasquez and Chris Vasil. The Pegasus Physicians at Stanford, a writers' group, tremendously shaped my book. Thanks to Drs. Lauren Edwards, Bruce Feldstein, Shaili Jain, William Meffert, Larissa Miyachi, Kendra Peterson, Noga Leah Ravid, Ali Tahvildari, and Clark Zhang for their support and feedback. I give special thanks to Drs. Mali Mann, Hans Steiner, and Irvin Yalom. Many thanks also to Drs. Diana Adams, Barbara Ballinger, Harvey Dondershine, Magdolna Dunai, Ellen Haller, Sharon Lipner, Terry Miller, Tom Nagy, Cynthia Nguyen, Mary Nichols, Patrick O'Neill, Patricia Paddison, Tom Plante, Randall Weingarten, and Daniel Winstead.

Giving speeches on this topic at the National Speaker's Association Pro-track Program immersed me in controversy and helped me create a dialogue that might transcend the polarization in our culture. In the Pro-track group, I met two brilliant writers who helped me with my book project: Lauren Mayer, also a humorist; and Mary Hanna. Their additions to this book are invaluable. I would also like to thank Jill Lublin and Scott Q. Marcus, whom I met through the National Speaker's Association.

I can't thank Rebecca Hall enough for her wonderful writing, editing, and incredible organizational skills. I feel lucky to have found someone so talented and dependable. Published author Jennifer duBois made time in her busy schedule for several extremely important critiques of my book. Amanita Rosenbush edited a previous version of this book, and some of her editing remains. Melissa Fairchild, LCSW, was kind enough to devote her time to improving my book as well.

I also want to thank the following authors for their generous time and support: Drs. Robert Cialdini, Helen Fisher, Philip Muskin, Terry Paulson, Barry Schwartz, and Deborah Tolman.

I worked on this book for years and, as I neared the end of the project, Valentine's Day 2015 gave me a final deadline. Thank you to everyone else who helped me to make this deadline: Ernesto Cuevas, Rachel Hanfling, Eric W. Peterson, Joanne Shwed, Kim Soderstrom, Emily Sper, Jim Thomsen, and Christina Tinling.

Many thanks to Peter Bowerman, Mark Duncan, John Eggen and Mission Marketing Mentors, and Pete Masterson for teaching me the details of publishing. I would also like to thank Ann and Dan Nitzan for their support and help with this project.

My dear friend, Vonni Serbin Contreary, and her wonderful husband, Kelvin; their children; Vonni's parents, Bob and Yvonne; and the whole Serbin family have showered me with inspiration, support, and much help with this book. Thank you for our longtime friendship and for sharing your expertise with flowers.

Emma (whose name was changed to protect her privacy) and her mother are very dear to me. Thanks for your wonderful friendship and inspiration.

My parents have supported me in this journey, even when they didn't understand it. My sister, Ann, shared her public relations skills with me, and they'll make this book more visible to the women who can benefit from it. Her generosity with her expertise in everything from design to marketing eased my journey writing this book.

And last but not least, I would like to thank my patients. In my psychiatric practice, my patients taught me why women across generations struggle with having a voice and standing up for themselves. To those women whom I will never meet, I hope this book will inspire you to find your voice.

Disclaimer

The intent of this book is to provide education and information related to psychology, relationships, and sex only. The information included in this book is provided and sold with the knowledge that the publisher and author do not offer any financial, medical, legal, or other professional advice, and this book is not intended to be an appropriate replacement or substitute for any such advice. No client-counselor relationship exists between you and any individual writing in this book. If any such advice is required, it is recommended to consult with the appropriate professional.

The intent of this book is to educate and entertain only. Any information included in this book might be dated. The author and publisher shall have no liability or responsibility to any person or entity regarding any loss or damage incurred, or alleged to have incurred, directly or indirectly, by the information included or referenced in this book.

This book does not include all information available on the subject. It is not the intent of this book to be specific to any individual's situation or needs. While every effort has been made to ensure the accuracy of this book, there may be typographical and or content errors. Therefore, this book should serve only as a general guide and not as the ultimate source of subject information.

Some names, characters, businesses, places, events, and incidents are either the products of the author's imagination or used in a fictitious manner. Some names and identifying details have been changed to protect the privacy of individuals.

You hereby agree to be bound by this disclaimer or, for a full refund, you may return this book within the allotted time period.

1

Why We Need a New Sexual Revolution: You Always Have a Choice

"One woman can change anything.
Many women can change everything."
—Gloria Steinem

Emma, the daughter of one of my dearest childhood friends, had recently started college. She called me for advice. "Susan, the guys are asking me to 'come over and hang out.' What does that mean?" she asked. I had no idea, but I figured it wasn't exactly an invitation to dinner and a movie. Did these guys want to be friends? Were they pursuing her romantically? Or was "hanging out" just another term for "hooking up"?

Emma wasn't interested in casual sex. As she soon learned, for many guys "hanging out" meant no-strings-attached intimacy. Unfortunately, at her college, there weren't many guys interested in taking a girl out to dinner and getting to know her, which was disappointing. Because she was careful about sex and held out for a guy to treat her with respect, Emma missed out on a lot of the fun of dating. As a result, she didn't learn about relationships or what she wanted in a partner. Most importantly, she didn't get the chance to find out about aspects of herself that she could only discover through dating.

I loved college dating, so this broke my heart. I began to wonder about what had happened to courtship and romance. Had dating become passé? Were cautious girls getting the short end of the stick when it came to guys? What would that mean for their futures? And Emma could not be the only one. There were many Emmas. This was not what we had in mind with the women's movement and the sexual revolution. We dreamed that women would be treated better when we were seen as equals, not that many men would simply take casual sex for granted. I was sad for my young friend, and I felt guilty that my generation, and the one before me, had inadvertently created this problem.

I saw that Emma was uncomfortable with modern dating—and rightly so. I also knew from my work as a psychiatrist that it wasn't just teenagers who were struggling. This was a problem for many women. I know, the word "psychiatrist" can make people uncomfortable—we are sometimes thought of as doctors for "crazy" people. But it just means I'm a doctor with medical and scientific training as well as experience working with patients. My practice includes a wide range of men and women, including those who just need some guidance building the life they want.

For years, I've helped women find individualized solutions to all kinds of problems—especially about dating, love, and sex. I've seen women of all ages who let men take them for granted and ended up confused and heartbroken. So when Emma said, "Susan, you have to do something about this," I realized that, as a psychiatrist and a single woman, I was in a unique position to figure out how we got here and what we can do about it.

What Do You Think?

1. Has being a "modern woman" worked for your love life?

2. When a "microwave romance" got too hot too quickly, did it explode in your face?

3. Could you tell whether he was into you, or did it feel like you were gambling with your heart?

It's time for a new sexual revolution. The old one didn't turn out the way we had hoped—especially for women. Instead of liberating ourselves, we've traded one unrealistic expectation (June Cleaver, 1950s TV perfect wife and mother) for another (Kim Kardashian, modern-day sex goddess). In today's culture of instant intimacy, with the old rule book long ago discarded, single women don't give themselves time to figure out whether guys can be trusted. Instead, we gamble with our emotions. We feel we're not supposed to complain about the risks because we're modern women. The truth is that we're making decisions based on what seems "politically correct" or what we think everyone else is doing. We often don't consider what's best for us emotionally. It's no wonder so many of us don't feel fully satisfied with our relationships.

It's time to be your own Brand of Sexy because one size doesn't fit all when it comes to dating. The women's movement and the sexual revolution were a huge leap forward for equality and freedom from inhibitions. Yet they set in motion a chain of events that turned upside down the way we date and relate. Now we're pioneers, trying to navigate a strange new territory without a map or a guide (or lots of conflicting maps and guides). We each need to develop a strong inner compass to help us navigate this journey. That means figuring out what you want, what works for you individually, and what strategies to use to achieve your relationship goals—whatever they may be.

3

Five Guidelines to Being Your Own Brand of Sexy

1. You always have a choice.

2. Media and peer pressure solutions might not be right for you.

3. Slow can be sexy.

4. Your voice matters.

5. If a guy isn't respecting your voice, move on.

Why Is It Valuable to Be Your Own Brand of Sexy?

1. You'll get clear about what's really important to you.

2. You'll improve your communication skills.

3. You'll feel better about yourself and improve your confidence.

4. You'll be more successful with men and dating, and enjoy the process more.

5. You'll be better able to tell whether or not he's into you.

6. You'll be better able to attract the right partner.

7. You'll gain the courage to say "no" to what you don't want.

We need a new sexual revolution that encourages each woman to decide what's best for her, regardless of the cultural expectations. Often being your own Brand of Sexy will require standing up to societal pressures, which can be intimidating. But, if women support each other in this, we can revolutionize dating. That way, all women—including you—can feel confident, comfortable, and in control. Being your own

Brand of Sexy and sisterhood are the keys to this revolution. I'll discuss all of this in more depth as the book continues.

Many women are conflicted about planning how to get what they want. Does it make you nervous to talk about strategies? In my psychiatric practice, I frequently hear patients say: "I don't want to play games" or "I don't want to seem manipulative." But it's not manipulative to refuse to accept being taken for granted. Meanwhile, other women are afraid that being "feminine" means being helpless and passive, and they don't want to give up their strength. Our challenge is to find a way to be strong *and* feminine.

Of course, many women are happy with their love lives. Perhaps they have instinctively found their own Brand of Sexy and, as a result, either they're enjoying a supportive, fulfilling relationship or they're truly content being single. If you are reading this book, however, it could be that you know you're not happy, or you have a vague feeling or fear that you've settled for less than you deserve. In either case, you need some new strategies to get what you want—and you've come to the right place. Being your own Brand of Sexy can help you to enjoy dating, whether you are navigating the dating scene later in life, a young woman trying to find her way in the college hookup culture, or anyone in between. Men who've read this book tell me that it's helped them create more meaningful relationships too, by helping them to better understand themselves and their partners. A new sexual revolution benefits us all.

I've been a board-certified psychiatrist in practice for 29 years, helping women who are confronting the same issues you are. My training in both psychological and biological issues gives me unique insight into how our bodies and feelings interact. And working with women of all ages has shown me how many of us are struggling with outdated patterns and expectations. I have put all that knowledge into this book to help you create your own personalized approach.

Now you're probably expecting me to share a personal story about my love life. Of course you expect it. We're in a let-it-all-hang-out, reality-TV, and Twitter culture! In fact, I've been told many times that I can't sell my book or this revolution without getting very personal. But it's complicated. Psychiatrists are trained not to reveal very much about themselves because, when people know too much about their psychiatrist, it can color that relationship in ways that can be a barrier to making progress. So, I prefer not to let it all hang out. But I can tell you that I'm just like you—a single, heterosexual woman who's also navigating the modern dating world. Being my own Brand of Sexy means retaining my privacy about the details of my personal life, and I have to honor what I feel is true to me. I want the same for you. Doing what feels right to you is a very important message of this book. And this book is about you, not me. I'm here to cheerlead you to do what's right for you.

After a wildly successful women's movement and the sexual revolution, many women are still people-pleasers who don't get what they want. I've been studying what works for my patients, my friends, and me for over 10 years now. I really enjoy dating. I've field-tested the strategies I share, so I know they work. My mission to share what I know has helped numerous women learn to enjoy dating and develop the relationships they want and deserve.

Owning Your Options

As a therapist, an author, and a woman, I support the choices you make on the road to becoming your happiest, best self. The first sexual revolution promised women more choices, but today cultural expectations still limit our options. I want more options because I understand that one will never be right for every woman. You will notice that I favor decisions that skew in one direction—decisions that have become less popular since the women's movement—because I believe that things like courtship and taking your time with intimacy can make dating a healthier and more fun experience. By encouraging these ideas, I'm not advocating that as a society we take away the dating strategies that I don't necessarily agree with. I support and accept women who choose different dating approaches than the ones I favor, as long as they are healthy choices.

That is the heart of sisterhood. It's about embracing each other's perspectives, even when they differ from our own. But sisterhood also involves caring about the outcome of your sisters' actions. And some of our sisters make choices that cause them a lot of pain. So I encourage women to avoid self-destructive behaviors that cause more heartache than good. For example, some women delude themselves into thinking they're OK with casual sex, even when it hurts them. Instead of telling them, "It's normal to feel that way, don't worry about it," a caring sister would say, "If this isn't good for you, don't do it." Rather than judging, let's help each other make more positive choices. Dating and relationships can be difficult, and supporting each other would help us all. As you grow, your own Brand of Sexy will evolve. Your needs and wants may change over time, along with what works for you. Support your sisters on their journey.

NOTE: Throughout this book I discuss sexuality in relation to heterosexual dynamics and norms. I support all sexualities; however, my clinical and personal area of expertise is in heterosexual relationships. Therefore, my focus here will be on relationships between men and women.

In each chapter I'll share stories about dating experiences. The premises should seem familiar because the stories are intended to illustrate common circumstances. They are designed to aid in your self-discovery, not to put a label on you. Your reaction to the stories ("Why did she care what her friends were doing? Why didn't she just slap him? I wish I could do something like that!") will help you recognize where your comfort level is with your own wants and needs and with the way men treat you.

In order to ensure the privacy of my patients, friends, and myself, the stories in this book are composites, taken from a variety of sources—work with patients, stories in magazines, talks with friends, and situations from my own life.

What Went Wrong?

> Laurel was dating Dan and hoped he'd bring up the subject of monogamy, but he never did, and her friends advised her not to scare him off. Still, Dan acted as if they were a couple, so Laurel was surprised when she ran into him with another woman. At first she was angry with him for what seemed like cheating on her, but she realized they'd never clarified whether or not they were "exclusive" before they had sex. She wondered, "I'm a modern woman. Why do I get so attached?"

Laurel's story is extremely common. In the past, the man was responsible for bringing up commitment, which eventually led to sex. Today there are no rules to guide us about how or when to broach this subject, leaving many couples in limbo about whether any expectations exist. And many women think it isn't OK to let your expectations be known because the "C" word is scary for men. But if women don't broach this subject, they often are vulnerable to unpleasant surprises. Many of us have lost the skill of protecting ourselves. Worse, many women see the feelings of attachment they experience with sex as the problem. But, as we'll see, we're built for attachment. We're simply no longer honoring the way we're built.

Wanting to be "normal" is human nature. We claim to prize our uniqueness, but part of us wants to be like everybody else. We often can't tell how much others influence us.[1] If we aren't careful, our media-saturated culture can pull us away from our true selves. We start to judge ourselves based on impossible standards and forget who we are in the process.

Most of us think the women's movement and the sexual revolution happened so long ago that we don't realize how much they shook up our culture. We're still figuring out how things have changed. In reality, it hasn't been that long since women made these astonishing gains. In fact, if I had been born 50 years earlier, I probably wouldn't have had the opportunity to become a psychiatrist.

Of course we needed change, but now it's time for a new sexual revolution. The old one didn't turn out the way we hoped—especially for women. We never imagined any drawbacks to sexual freedom. We threw out traditional rules as if they had no value and didn't replace them with a new roadmap to guide us. Now we are confused about which direction to go. We didn't realize we might be losing the armor we need to protect ourselves in this new world. And when so many of us are trying so hard to be sex objects, is that really "sexual freedom"?

Do you compare yourself with other women and come up short? Perhaps you have worried that you aren't attractive enough. Or maybe you feel so bad about how you look that you would spend a lot of money to solve your "problem." There's nothing new about women being valued for our physical traits. But, in our rush to ditch the old ideal, we just replaced it with an even more unrealistic one. Did sexual freedom trap us into a tyranny of external beauty?

Whether or not we are more image-obsessed than our preliberation counterparts, new cosmetic procedures reinforce these unrealistic expectations. And we now have the money to spend on them. Americans spent $10.7 billion on cosmetic procedures in 2010, and over 92 percent of that was by women.[2] It's no surprise that women struggle more with body image than men, which author Caitlin Moran says is due to "women's continuing demented belief that, at any moment, they might face some snap inspection of their 'total hotness.'"[3] Most of us feel the need to be "sex objects," not just to attract a man but to meet our own standards and to compete with other women. (Too often, women want to be skinnier than most men would find attractive.)[4] Women wouldn't go this far to be sex objects without some sort of societal pressure.

Liberation was exciting and necessary, but we wanted so much to break free that we never envisioned the sacrifice involved, for ourselves or future generations. Things have improved a great deal from the old days. Today, women have more options. Sex is no longer shameful or unspeakable. But in the process of change, we gave up protections that we'd taken for granted, like chivalry and courtship. Plus, in asserting our independence, we no longer expect as much from men—and it shows.[5] We now chase the bad boys, and we don't require them to commit. Maybe we no longer want paternalistic protection, but do we really want to give up expecting men to be accountable for their actions?

It's great that we lost the stigma surrounding sex. But even though the expectation of virginity restricted us, it also protected us. The rituals of courtship meant that women could wait to see how a man treated them before they got physically (and emotionally) invested. Women used to want—and hold out for—emotional connection, not casual sex. Now we are tolerating behaviors that would *never* have been acceptable in the past. Men didn't invite women over to "hang out" if they hardly knew them nor did they expect casual sex on the first date. It's the "new math": Sex = Power. In other words, many of us think that the more sex we have, the more empowered we are, even if we don't feel completely comfortable with it.

It's time to re-examine what works for us as individuals. Sure, there are women who really are fine with casual hook-ups. But, for most of us, sex is still not separate from intimacy, despite what we think ought to be "normal." And, even if you don't want to be a sex goddess like Kim Kardashian, you or somebody you know has probably experienced the pressure to have sex before you're ready. With unprecedented freedoms, it's critical for individuals to know what's right for them rather than to simply follow the crowd.

What Isn't Working?

> Priya really hit it off with Steve at a party. He even found an excuse to give her his phone number, but she was disappointed he never asked her for her number. Some of her friends said to forget him: "If he doesn't pursue you, he's not that into you." But other friends told her, "Stop being uptight and just ask him out." Eventually she called him even though she was ambivalent about making the first move. They decided to meet for coffee and had another great conversation. At the end of the date, he said, "Let's do this again. Call me." Frustrated, Priya remembered the last time she felt this way with a guy—it felt like she was pursuing him and was never sure how interested he was. But could this guy be different? Was she being too passive if she let this one go?

Have you ever bought self-help books about dating? Or asked friends for advice? You may have noticed that the advice was frequently contradictory. (The experts are pioneers just like you are, and we're all trying to find our way in this new territory.) More importantly, have you ever longed for more romance and courtship but wondered if that was old-fashioned?

One of the biggest casualties of the sexual revolution was romance. We aren't sure if equality means there are no differences between men and women. So, men aren't sure how much courtship is required (or even desired), and women aren't sure it's OK to want romance. Women are still more likely than men to struggle with being their own Brands of Sexy because we are often conditioned to be people-pleasers. Still, many men face these problems too. In fact, men frequently complain that they don't know what women want. Does he open the door for her or does that imply she's helpless? Does he help her put on her coat or is that too old-fashioned?

It's confusing for everyone. Many of us aren't sure if it's OK to need a commitment before having sex or to expect the guy to pick up the check. Some of us are trying so hard to be "normal" that we've let societal changes shake our confidence until we're not sure what we really want. And some of us have embraced the masculine in ourselves to the point that we don't realize when we're pushing men away (when we do the chasing). Without societal rules, it becomes more important than ever for us to develop our own sense of what is best for us emotionally. Our choices are limited when we accept cultural norms over the value of knowing ourselves.

The women's movement bonded us together toward a common goal. But, when it was over, we took our newfound freedoms and went our separate ways. We have forgotten that we're still in the same boat together. We've moved to separate corners on many issues: Should you play hard to get or is that playing games? Which is best: abstinence-only education or comprehensive sex education? The fighting can get mighty bloody. Must there be a winner and a loser? Do we really want a cookie-cutter approach? The women's movement championed the cause of choices for women. We certainly don't want to develop a culture where only one choice (casual sex) is available. Perhaps our lack of unity is part of the problem.

After fighting so hard to have the power to be individuals, women are no longer celebrating those differences. When we say our way is better, the implication is "Your way is no good" rather than "Maybe your way is right for you." We're in trouble when we ignore who we truly are and when our sisters no longer support us in expressing that individuality.

Without clear guidelines, many women have trouble saying "no" to what they don't want and are more likely to give in to societal pressures. That often isn't ideal in an overly sexualized culture. We need to change things because we've lost the rules that guided relationships, we've lost societal protections, and we've lost the value we placed on romance and connectedness. As a result, modern dating just isn't working for many of us. What can we do to regain what we've lost without returning to the 1950s?

Why We Need a New Sexual Revolution

> Jennifer is a confident, successful, 38-year-old executive on her first date with a cute new guy. They start grooving to the live band, and suddenly he starts dancing suggestively and puts his hand on her derriere. Jennifer doesn't like it, so she moves away and suggests they sit this one out.

> Talia is an 18-year-old college freshman, thrilled to finally get invited to a party at the frat house with all the cute guys. The hottie she's dancing with begins to touch her and grind against her but, when she looks around, everyone else in the room is dancing that way. Talia feels horribly uncomfortable, but she wants to be cool so she gets invited back, and she starts to think, "What's wrong with me that I don't like this?"

Why do you think Jennifer finds it easier than Talia to be her own Brand of Sexy? Are these two stories just examples of extremes of confidence? Age difference? Peer pressure? Or is the difference also in the environment? Most of us are in the middle of the spectrum from completely passive to supremely confident. We'd like to think we have it all figured out, but many of us don't.

Modern life bombards us with sexual imagery. Sex sells, so it's reflected everywhere: in TV, in print, and online. Naturally, we want to be "normal," so we question ourselves. "How much sex is normal? If I have it less than four times a week, is there something wrong with me? What's wrong with me that I can't find a boyfriend? Do I need to lose weight or get breast implants?" The saturation of sex in our culture pressures us to look and act sexy or sexual, causing us to confuse our value with our sexuality.

These days, parents worry (for good reason) about the sexualization of their daughters. When stores sell skimpy t-shirts for 10-year-olds that say JAIL BAIT, commercials and billboards ooze sex, and characters on sitcoms hop in and out of bed, it's hard for parents to help their girls feel good about who they are as people, not just the sum of how they look or dress, or how much sex they're having. It takes honesty and courage to realize when a trend is not right for you, but you also need the ability to stand up for yourself. If you realize it's not working for you and still go along with it, you aren't being true to yourself.

In the past, women didn't have much trouble saying "no" to sex. A man truly felt he "got lucky" if a woman would have sex with him. It wasn't just a cute expression, and society supported women in withholding sex. Today we have to be able to say "no" without support from our culture. Of course, the consequences of opting out of sexual mores was much more severe in the past. Many young women today say, "Modern women should be able to date and have casual sex. What's wrong with me that I get so attached?" If we are doing things that we're uncomfortable with because our culture seems to demand it, we are not truly liberated.

The more young women experience this overly sexual culture, the more some will accept it as "just the way it is." If we accept it as the norm, we put girls and women at greater risk of being touched, leered at, or groped. Maybe reports of sexual assaults and harassment have declined,[6,7] but many women simply avoid places like dance clubs where grinding and touching are "normal" because complaining is so difficult when you're in the minority.

We need a *new* sexual revolution because we've lost the rules that guided relationships, leaving us confused about the game of love. We've lost the value we placed on romance and connectedness. Many of us have convinced ourselves that our value is in our sexual appeal. Without societal protections, it becomes more important than ever for us to develop our own sense of what is best for us emotionally—to be our own Brands of Sexy. We each need to protect ourselves because one size will never fit everyone.

Let's not forget what we learned from the women's movement. Before then, some women blindly accepted the roles that culture assigned them without even recognizing when societal norms were leading them to unfulfilled and unhappy lives, and others felt powerless to change the situation. Believe it or not, we aren't so different today. We've simply replaced one set of unrealistic norms for another. We feel we have no choice because it's "just the way it is." We don't stop to ask what is best for us as individuals because we're too busy trying to fit in. But we do have a choice—we can join together and start a new sexual revolution that allows each of us to break free of those unrealistic cultural norms and be our own Brands of Sexy.

Saying "no" is incredibly difficult, especially for women. We want to please people. And sometimes when a girl says "no," a guy *will* be angry. But even that situation *could* be a confidence booster, *if* she can value the act of standing up for herself and see his reaction as *his* problem, rather than some fault of her own.

Julie is at a salsa club dancing with Ian, who's a friend of the friends she came with and seems like a nice guy. She's thinking what a great dancer he is when suddenly Ian runs his hands up her legs to her hips, which makes her extremely uncomfortable. Trying to be diplomatic, Julie says with a smile, "Uh, what's with the hands?" Ian teasingly says, "What are you, a virgin?" She says, "What does that have to do with it?" and he apologizes.

Standing your ground is a lesson for us all. In my practice, I see how setting boundaries transforms lives. We like to blame the media for society's problems, but we influence our culture's sexuality too. Each of us, teenagers as well as adults, needs to learn how to speak up for ourselves in a constructive way. Knowledge and confidence are far sexier than bare midriffs and cleavage. It's up to us to redefine what it means to be sexy, feminine, powerful women, and this definition may look different for each of us. We need to respect those differences and give women permission to do what's right for each of us. Together, we can create a new revolution and stand up to cultural expectations that aren't working for us.

Learning to Be Your Own Brand of Sexy

After Nina had her heart broken yet again by another guy who seemed like he was into her but didn't call, Nina finally decided it worked better for her to wait until the guy asked her out. She wanted to take her time getting emotionally and physically involved. Sure, she may have had fewer Friday night dates, but Nina figured that, if they weren't into her enough to make a little effort, she was better off without them. Holding out for better treatment from men helped her regain her power. She felt so good about protecting herself emotionally that she felt better, even though she wasn't having sex. Several months later, along came Tim. He really liked her, actively pursued her, and wanted a real relationship. They're still together, happily hiking into the sunset.

Maybe you wouldn't handle your love life the way Nina did, but we each have to be our own Brand of Sexy. That means doing what's best for us emotionally, not doing something just to please a guy, or our friends, or because everyone else is doing it. But a new sexual revolution doesn't mean we have to demonstrate or burn bras. We just need to figure out what works for us. Then we can hold out for guys who respect us and treat us well.

A new sexual revolution is the understanding that we are different from one another. We are beautiful in our differences, just as each type of flower has its own unique beauty. (Nobody tells a lily, "Your petals are too fat.") Let's take what we learned from the last women's movement and the sexual revolution and move forward. The women's movement challenged the belief that women are all alike and inferior to men. Why would we want to replace those old judgmental attitudes ("What's wrong with her that she's not a virgin?") with new, equally judgmental ones ("What's wrong with her that she is a virgin?")? Do we have to act certain ways to be "modern"? Do we really believe that we're still all alike and that our individual needs don't matter? Despite our new freedom, we are not celebrating our individuality. Instead, we've traded in one unrealistic role model for another—the June Cleaver/Kim Kardashian paradox. We've gone from thinking we should aspire to be the perfect wife and mother to believing we should be the perfect sex object.

Change is challenging, especially in a world so polarized by our differences. But a new sexual revolution involves acceptance rather than judgment and endless loops of arguments. It's OK to be different. Acceptance of our differences was the goal we wanted to achieve with the women's movement. We now need to work together to find workable solutions by understanding our differences and vulnerabilities. We can achieve this through a new sexual revolution that is founded in being your own Brand of Sexy and sisterhood. The most effective way for women to have power on a societal level is when we all stick together. If enough of us stopped letting men get away with bad behavior, many of these men would be forced to change.

If your heart's been bruised, you might not feel powerful enough to think you can change. Believe it or not, those disappointing experiences could teach you a great deal. In fact, if you've experienced enough trial and error in love, you might be able to begin to spot patterns. That could help you figure out if you're repeating certain mistakes. But don't worry if you haven't learned from those mistakes yet. You're about to see what isn't working for you and how a new sexual revolution can help.

The How-Tos of the New Sexual Revolution—
Being Your Own Brand of Sexy and Sisterhood

Over the next several chapters, I will discuss why we need a new sexual revolution and how we can start one. Rather than making strict new rules, we can join together in sisterhood to establish dating guidelines and suggestions that many women will be able to support and implement. These changes can improve your love life, and I'll show you how. The first step is being your own Brand of Sexy.

To review, here are the five guidelines to being your own Brand of Sexy:

1. **You always have a choice.**
   We'll discuss how to determine what is best for you and how to go about achieving that.

2. **Media and peer pressure solutions might not be right for you.**
   We'll get clarity about the influences—society, friends, and family—that make it harder for you to do what's best for you because media and peer pressure solutions might not be right for you.

3. **Slow can be sexy.**
   The value of protecting yourself emotionally is often overlooked in today's dating culture. We'll discuss why slow can be sexy and how to guard your heart.

4. **Your voice matters.**
   We'll discuss the importance of expressing yourself because your voice matters. You'll learn about the Single Woman's 12-Piece Dating Toolbox, a dozen tools to help you navigate modern dating and find your voice. You'll have an opportunity to "try on" different types of dating styles while not ignoring potential "sand traps and pitfalls."

5. **If a guy isn't respecting your voice, move on.**
   You deserve to find a man who is looking for the same type of relationship as you and who will respect your boundaries. If you've communicated your needs and he still doesn't treat you with respect, then move on.

Sisterhood

Being your own Brand of Sexy is crucial, but it isn't enough for a new sexual revolution to take place. We also need to support each other in finding our own Brands of Sexy. We need sisterhood. We'll discuss how sisterhood can provide value for you today in the following chapters.

Along this journey, you'll learn how women and men *are* different, but the reasons why are less important than figuring out what to do about it. We'll examine how to reintroduce romance without going back to the '50s and the importance of sharpening your instincts and intuition. By the end of the book, you'll have a better sense of what works for you as an individual and how to get it.

In reality, sex *doesn't* equal power. Knowledge is power. Self-worth is power. Being your own Brand of Sexy is power. We need a new sexual revolution because it's time to redefine what it means to be sexy, feminine, powerful women. Women and men have changed the world many times before, and we can do it again—one date at a time.

2

Media and Peer Pressure Solutions
Might Not Be Right for You

*"The more things change,
the more they stay the same."*
—Alphonse Karr

A s we saw in Chapter 1, the reason we need a new sexual revolution is that the old one simply traded one set of unrealistic standards for another. Let's face it: Our mothers and grandmothers couldn't live up to the shining example of June Cleaver as "perfect" wives and mothers. Today we can't live up to the idealized image of Kim Kardashian's "out there" sex-goddess persona.

Without the old rules in place, both men and women are confused about dating. As Deborah L. Tolman, San Francisco State University Professor of Human Sexuality Studies, said in *The New York Times*, "When girls and young women are more than ever socialized to be the best 'sex objects' they can be, is it surprising that women grow up struggling to know what they want?"[8]

Don't get me wrong. Many remarkable benefits resulted from the sexual revolution. The women's movement led to huge improvements in women's freedom and rights too. Most of us don't want to return to the 1950s. The women's movement helped women understand that they were conforming to societal norms at the expense of their individuality. The norms have changed today. Interestingly, many of us are *still* conforming rather than doing what's best *for us*.

Despite its importance, society has yet to take on this issue. Back in 2005, *The New York Times* columnist Maureen Dowd wrote: "Before it was don't be a sex object; now it's be a sex object—but the conformity is just as stifling."[9]

Wanting to be "normal" is simply human nature. Although we claim to want to be unique, part of us wants to be like everybody else. At the same time, we often can't tell how much we're being influenced by others. As we become more aware of the societal pressures we face, we are strengthened as a result and empowered to free ourselves from their spells. Without awareness, we don't recognize we are part of a herd—like sheep—just following the crowd.

Social psychologists have demonstrated how people can blindly follow others. In 1969, a study was done by social psychologist Stanley Milgram and his colleagues involving people in Manhattan. They found that, when just one person stopped on a busy New York City sidewalk and looked up, people ignored the behavior. When five people were looking up, four times as many people stopped.[10] In this simple situation, we can easily recognize that the subjects look up because everyone else is doing it. In more complex situations, however, the influence is not so obvious.

Robert B. Cialdini, author of *Influence: Science and Practice,* says, "The principle of social proof asserts that people, especially when they are unsure of themselves, follow the lead of similar others."[11] He believes this explains everything from the power of product testimonials to the increased incidence of copycat suicides and mass murders after highly publicized similar incidents. Cialdini argues that the power of these sorts of automatic human responses is hard for us to perceive. This makes us vulnerable to the influence of others. Studies show that people often minimize how often other people's behavior affects their own.[12]

Ashley feels she is a typical teen. She makes decent grades and stays out of trouble. She used to shop at the hip stores, just like her friends. Life was good. Then a financial setback required Ashley's family to cut up the credit cards. Ashley was not allowed to buy anything new. Rather than be embarrassed, Ashley made excuses when her friends went to the mall. She stayed home and spent time with her parents, who were living a stripped-down existence without cable TV, Internet, and cell phones.

At first, Ashley felt out of it when her friends showed up at school with their new sexy t-shirts that said, BUY ME THINGS AND I'LL BE NICER and I TAUGHT YOUR BOYFRIEND THAT THING YOU LIKE on the front. She searched for something similar at Goodwill but couldn't find anything. She settled for an embroidered peasant blouse that reminded her of her Mom's college pictures. The next day, wearing her $3 blouse, Ashley was stopped in the hallway at school. That cute boy she'd had her eye on said, "Hey, Ash! Nice outfit. I had you pegged for one of those crowd-followers. Glad you decided to rock your own style."

Since Ashley's new style developed purely out of necessity, it seems unlikely that she's escaped the desire to dress like her friends. Will the cute guy's enthusiasm for her new look help her appreciate the futility of living for the opinions of others? Or will she just be confused about which look is best? Although teenagers like Ashley are particularly vulnerable to the pressure to conform, society's influence doesn't seem to diminish as we get older.

Women in particular are socialized to be people-pleasers. And because women are generally less confident than men— the "confidence gap"—women are more vulnerable to pressures from others.[13] We often do what others expect from us to the point of denying our own needs. This is how our culture can pull us away from our true selves. Being a people-pleaser steeped in a culture that emphasizes sex, youth, and beauty can drive a desire to be a sex object (at any age). Older women feel invisible, younger women lose sight of what works for them as individuals, and mothers are scared to raise daughters in a world where clothing stores offer t-shirts labeled JAIL BAIT for 10-year-olds. And none of us will get treated well unless we're strong enough to be our own Brand of Sexy, instead of simply yielding to social pressure. As we saw in Chapter 1, being your own Brand of Sexy means doing what is best for you as an individual by following these five guidelines:

1. You always have a choice.

2. Media and peer pressure solutions might not be right for you.

3. Slow can be sexy.

4. Your voice matters.

5. If a guy isn't respecting your voice, move on.

Explosive Changes: The Old Revolutions

Most of us know the amazing benefits of the women's movement and the sexual revolution. For those of us who grew up later than the 1960s, it's hard to believe that just a few decades ago employers wouldn't hire women for most professional jobs and no one discussed sex openly. Women went to college to get an MRS degree and were "old maids" if they were single at the old age of (gasp) 25.

Then, in the early 1960s, Betty Friedan wrote *The Feminine Mystique*. She described "the problem with no name"—the vague discontent of educated women who felt limited to supporting their husbands' and children's lives instead of building their own.[14] She blamed society for these expectations. Friedan helped give women a whole new perspective and encouraged them to demand more freedom and choices. Around that time, the birth control pill fueled the sexual revolution. It freed women from unwanted pregnancy, which often had dire consequences. Before the pill, you were shamed if you had premarital sex. An unplanned pregnancy could derail your life. Your choices were few: have a shotgun wedding, hide away during the pregnancy and then give your child up for adoption, or face harsh societal judgment. Abortions were illegal and very dangerous.

The young people of the 1960s created change in every arena, from politics to music, fashion to dating. Women gained new rights and freedoms. Premarital sex was no longer taboo. In fact, sex wasn't just out in the open. It was everywhere!

Sex Sells

Because of these radical changes, advertisers cashed in on the power of sex as a marketing tool. Sex went from a hush-hush topic to something the media shouted in a deafening roar, blasting us with sexually explicit images. Peggy Orenstein described the resulting problem in *Cinderella Ate My Daughter: Dispatches from the Front Lines of the New Girlie-Girl Culture*: "It is easy to become impervious to shock, to adjust to each new normal—even brief exposures to stereotypes in advertisements, TV shows, and the like unconsciously increase women's and girls' acceptance of them."[15]

After 50 years of increasingly scandalous media, the more we see sexual images, the more we think "it's no big deal," and the more explicit they must be to get our attention. Miley

Cyrus's 2013 "good girl gone bad" shocker is a prime example. Timed to occur with the release of her new album, her MTV Video Music Awards performance gained widespread publicity because it was so risqué.[16] Her equally sexual music video, *Wrecking Ball*, was so over the top that it was banned from French daytime TV.[17]

Our exposure to media has also exploded with 24/7 access, promoting a "talk-show culture." These days, sexuality spreads like wildfire, and we're expected to air our dirty laundry for the world to hear. In fact, sex plus media is a new recipe for fame. Paris Hilton and Kim Kardashian both became celebrities after the release of widely viewed sex tapes. Of course, people have always had wild sexual exploits. But, until recently, everything was kept under wraps. These days, people tweet about it!

We've gained the freedom that we wanted and needed. But there's a downside we didn't anticipate and we often don't recognize. When the gains were so big for women, it's hard for us to find fault with these changes. Most of us don't want to return to 1950s rules, but it's important to look at those unintended outcomes to see the big picture, so we can figure out where we want to go next.

Something Gained, Something Lost

Because of her good looks, Marnie manages to land a job as a hostess in a nice club. There, she runs into the successful, attractive man she's been drooling over. He insists she leave right then so they can go have sex. Though she initially protests that she's at work, the next time we see her they're on their way to his place. The only foreplay we see is at his place, when he shows her his art. After weeks of being together, he invites her to be his hostess for the party he's having at his home. She's thrilled. While she's basking in the glow of coupledom at the party, he offers her $500 for her help. "You don't have to pay me. I'm your girlfriend," she says.[18] "I didn't realize I had a girl-friend," he replies.[19] In response to her shock, he says that his last assistant slept with him, but at least she "got" the relationship.[20]

If this story seems familiar, perhaps you've seen the HBO series *Girls*, where courtship is a thing of the past, and protection means condoms and the pill.[21] There is no talk of protecting your heart in this show; being battered and bruised from potholes and rocks on the path are simply an expected part of the journey.

Yes, we needed to change the old-fashioned dating rules that were overly rigid and limited our options. But we simply threw them out without learning how to protect ourselves emotionally in our newly liberated culture. In fact, we went one step further than discarding all dating rules. We replaced the old rules with new cultural expectations that aren't always in our best interest, like the idea that women will have sex before commitment. We gave up protections that we took for granted, that we never dreamed we'd miss. As a result, we lost clarity and left ourselves exposed to emotionally risky situations, like Marnie's. Establishing new dating guidelines that are focused on how to be our own Brands of Sexy can emotionally protect us. They can help us stand up to pressures that don't work for us, so that we can enjoy the freedom of modern dating in a healthier way.

Without rules, dating can feel like we're navigating a brand new world without a compass. Sexual freedom can be confusing. Have you ever wondered if a guy was really into you? Or wondered how long to wait to have sex? Have you ever worried that a guy expected sex right away and might disappear if you wouldn't sleep with him? We can end up feeling taken for granted when popular culture tells us that having lots of sex is "normal," rather than emphasizing the importance of being treated well by men.

To make things even more complex, the double standard is alive and well despite equality and sexual freedom. Too many men and women both expect that women will have sex early on and don't respect women who give it up quickly. Marnie found this out the hard way. He expected sex immediately, and then treated her like an employee rather than a girlfriend. The word "slut" seems to be eternal. The idea that women should be looked down upon if they have casual sex still exists, despite the women's movement and the sexual revolution. If we want to have sex soon into the relationship, we often worry that the guy won't take us seriously as girlfriend material if we do.

Without guidelines, dating is more and more confusing and marriage is not always the goal. And, although we'd like to believe what others do sexually doesn't affect us, University of Texas at Austin Associate Professor of Sociology Mark Regnerus, one of the authors of *Premarital Sex in America: How Young Americans Meet, Mate, and Think about Marrying*, begs to differ. He says: "If a critical mass of men and women enjoy an extended series of sexual relationships and expect sex fairly promptly within them, it becomes quite difficult for a minority to do otherwise."[22] Sexual economics theory says that the economics of the marketplace (the dating scene) greatly affects every date you have. We're talking about the principles of competition and supply and demand. If there are tons of women who want casual sex before they decide if that person is boyfriend material, then it's harder for you (or a guy who doesn't want casual sex) to hold out and remain competitive. If this is where we're headed, it gives many women fewer choices.

The same is true of commitment. When less people want commitment, it is harder to find a partner to commit. This can require you to pay a higher price (make more compromises). If "commitment phobia" seems like an epidemic, it's not your imagination. Marriage rates have dropped greatly.[23] In 1950, more than 75 percent of adults were married. Today, fewer than half are. This is a historic low, and it continues to drop. Single women have more than 50 percent of the babies born to women under 30.[24] The old rules of placing a premium on marriage no longer apply.

The Rise of the Hookup Culture and the Demise of Romance—The Confusion of Casual Sex and How Slow Can Be Sexy

> Keisha meets some friends for drinks, and a cute guy starts flirting with her. When Mark offers to drive Keisha home, her friends are thrilled for her. Keisha is concerned that he might just want a hookup, which she's not sure she wants. Her friends say, "What's the problem? He's really hot!" and encourage her to go for it. When they get to Keisha's place, she decides to invite Mark in, and they have a great time until the alcohol wears off a little and she begins to have second thoughts. He accepts it when she puts the brakes on their makeout session, and even calls her afterward to get together. But he suggests bringing a video over to her place. It's clear he wants to start up where they left off, on the couch in a liplock. She'd rather have a do-over and go on a real date, but she feels awkward bringing it up at this point.

Keisha isn't the only young woman who is confused by the modern "hookup culture," in which it seems like everyone is jumping in and out of each other's beds. Part of the difficulty is that it's very hard to get accurate statistics about sexual activity. It's a sensitive topic to begin with, and researchers have to rely on respondents' self-reporting, which often isn't reliable. (This may explain that so-called study someone at the office heard of, claiming "happy couples have sex five times a week.")

So let's take the following statistics with a grain of salt: According to the most recent *National Health Statistics Report*, 60 percent of men and 76 percent of women ages 15-44 have had six or fewer sexual partners in their lifetime.[25] In the most recent year for which statistics are available, only 18 percent of men and 15 percent of women (ages 15-44) had more than one partner all year.[26] Looks pretty tame, compared to the impression we get from TV shows! Is it possible that people don't have nearly as many sexual partners as we might think? Is the hookup culture a battle of the sexes in which women want commitment and men want sex? Or do some men want commitment and some women want sex? Or does it simply give women new power over their sexuality? It's probably all of the above, depending on the woman and man involved.

One thing seems certain: Women don't experience as much pleasure as men do during casual sexual encounters. Academic research shows that the "orgasm gap" described by Stanford sociologist Paula England is even greater in casual sex.[27] Women experience orgasm during hookups only half as often as men. Another interesting fact: Men perform oral sex only 50 percent of the time during first-time hookups. Women are more generous, offering oral sex 80 percent of the time.[28]

The goal of the sexual revolution was acceptance of sexuality rather than feeling ashamed, which led to much more casual sex. But casual sex doesn't work for everyone. Yet many women feel they must experience sex and be "good at it" without *any* sexual inhibitions. In a world filled with people trying to be "normal" (whatever that means!), in a culture saturated with sex, there can be a fine line between giving permission to be sexual and persuading others to be sexual. Keisha's friends could have said, "Do what's comfortable for you," which would have encouraged her intuition and self-knowledge; instead, they encouraged her to be sexual and to discount her own reservations. If Keisha is easily influenced by others, this approach can create problems for her.

When we decide hooking up is all we want or need, we are saying that romance is no longer necessary. How does this loss of romance change the dynamic of relationships in general—not just one-night stands?

Trina meets Ivan through friends and they instantly click. As a modern woman, Trina is comfortable asking Ivan out and they begin to see each other regularly. Ivan clearly enjoys her company but he doesn't make much effort to see her—that doesn't bother Trina; she doesn't believe in playing games, and she isn't big on the "hearts and flowers" romance stuff. Pretty soon they fall into a weekend routine—Ivan comes over, Trina cooks dinner, he washes her car, and they spend the evening reading books in bed. After a few months of this, Trina wants to change the dynamic. She wants Ivan to take the initiative and plan some dates. He makes an effort for a while, and then returns to his old ways. But he's a great guy, and she always wanted a boyfriend—so why is she so dissatisfied?

Trina and Ivan's relationship lacks romance—she may not need hearts and flowers but, when she makes all the plans, she feels less like a girlfriend and more like his mommy. It might have seemed logical for her to initiate the relationship, but it didn't work for her emotionally. Two of the biggest casualties of the sexual revolution have been romance and courtship. Many women would prefer a guy to take the initiative. They'd like to be pursued, but they're not sure it's OK to want that because it's "old-fashioned." And holding out for a commitment or marriage feels practically medieval to some. When it's difficult to stand up for what we truly want, we risk convincing ourselves that we're wrong to want it.

We're not sure if equality means most men and women are supposed to be the same. So, men aren't sure how much courtship they should offer. Believe it or not, a guy might be chewed out for opening a door for his date. Today's women aren't sure it's OK to want romance—but, if you do want it, you're not alone. Look at the sale of romance novels—they comprise more than a third (the largest share) of all popular fiction sold.[29] People may mock "chick lit" and "bodice rippers," but those books make serious profits—$1.4 billion in sales a year, and Harlequin sells four books per second.[30,31] Fictional romance is more popular than ever before, even through economic downturns. Could this large market indicate that many women are hungry for the romance they're missing in real life? Or is their sexual content the big draw? Or could it be both?

In today's culture, courtship seems so dated—but do you secretly still yearn for it? Perhaps you feel you're supposed to pretend that as a "modern woman" you don't need that sort of thing. With the old rules cast aside, many of us feel we no longer need to worry about protecting our hearts, so we aren't taking that time. We've forgotten that slow can be sexy. We get emotionally involved before we know much about the guy, and we aren't immune to attachment when we have sex. When we don't safeguard ourselves on an emotional level, we can feel powerless, and we're often left confused, frustrated, or even heartbroken when things don't go well. Because, despite all the changes, for many women and men sex is still not separate from intimacy and a real relationship with a partner. Sex actually *doesn't* equal power, so we need all new ways to protect ourselves without losing the option to have sex before marriage or returning to the rule of virginity.

We're discovering that men and women are different and have different needs. And women aren't all the same either. As we learned in the '60s, some women did want to stay home and be wives and mothers. We want choices, options, and possibilities—so we can do what works best for each of us.

One of the biggest consequences of all these changes is that we've lost a bit of our humanity. When we think sex equals power, we marginalize emotional intimacy. As we will see in Chapter 4, human beings are built for connection. Our brains need consistent bonding and nurturing, and studies have shown that babies and children don't thrive without contact and touch. Do you remember how it felt when you lost someone you loved to a breakup or worse? Chances are that you had trouble sleeping, that you lost interest in everything else. It disrupted your body's rhythms. Frequent breakups aren't just emotionally painful, they put your body on a physiological roller coaster ride. We need connections, and we don't outgrow that need when we grow up.

Men Are Struggling Too

It's Saturday night and Josh is all dressed up for his office party, which has nearly 100 attendees. An attractive female coworker is flirting with him. They've had a few drinks, and she's getting friendlier. She whispers in his ear what she would like to do to him. He doesn't know what to do. Is she just flirting and a little drunk? If he turns her down, will she tell people at the office he's gay? Will he have to act as if he's repulsed by her to save face since we believe men never turn down casual sex?

Despite how times have changed, many men still feel masculinity has certain requirements. Just as women have been conditioned by society to play a certain role, men also have a script. More men than ever before have broken out of those old stereotypes, but they still exist. Just as women still feel pressure to be "feminine" (pretty, sweet, helpless, passive, dependent, and considerate of others' feelings), many men still feel they must be strong, independent, aggressive, sexual, productive, logical, and adventurous to be masculine.

And they must avoid emotional vulnerability. In a way, they're caught in the same bind we are—trying to discover how to be *their* own Brands of Sexy in the face of cultural pressure to conform.

Without the old rules, men also struggle to figure out what works for them as individuals. For instance, a woman offers to pay on dates, testing to see whether the guy will agree. When he does, he's failed a test because he was trying to do what he thought his date wanted. On the one hand, we might think "men have it easy." When they pull anything outrageous, we say that "boys will be boys." And they can get away with far worse behavior than women. But there is a flip side. Men are still expected to be sexual, aggressive beings who enjoy the challenge of conquering women and who—unlike our friend Josh—would never shy away from an opportunity to have sex.

In *The End of Men: And the Rise of Women,* author Hanna Rosin says men are still "backing away from what were more traditionally feminine traits as women take over more masculine ones."[32] We have evolved into "Plastic Woman" and "Cardboard Man," Rosin says. Plastic Woman has become adept at performing "superhuman feats of flexibility." She brings home the bacon and fries it up in a pan, all while diapering the baby and typing her master's thesis. In contrast, Rosin's "Cardboard Man" is stuck in neutral. He is confused that the roles of breadwinner and head of the family are no longer his domain alone. A man may even feel that being hit on by a woman takes away his masculinity. What if he prefers to be the aggressor? What if he sees her as a "slut"? Or, like Josh in the example above, what if he just isn't interested?

The Tyranny of Beauty and the Power of Sisterhood

Jane is a stunning woman with a fabulous figure. But, no matter how beautiful she looks, she is always finding fault with her appearance. If someone compliments her on her lovely skin or her terrific outfit, she points out a couple of tiny blemishes or claims that the dress would look way better if she could lose 10 pounds. There is no shortage of men who find her attractive and ask her out, but the relationships never seem to work out. After the last guy fizzles out, Jane decides she won't be able to keep a boyfriend until she has liposuction and a chemical peel.

Have you ever known someone like Jane? Or have you ever had those kinds of thoughts about yourself? It's hard not to get down on ourselves when it comes to appearance. We are constantly bombarded by airbrushed images of perfect-looking models. And gorgeous actresses who actually look like normal-sized women are blasted for being "fat." Plus, the difference between "normal" and "ideal" has exploded in recent years. In the 1950s, the average mannequin had the same hip measurements as the average woman. By 1990 there was a 6-inch difference between the hips of mannequins and the hips of the average woman.[33] Even as recently as 1992, models only weighed 8 percent less than the typical American woman. But, over the past two decades, models have gotten dramatically thinner even as average weights have gone up. These days, models weigh 23 percent less than most women and are also much taller.[34] The average woman is 5'4" and weighs 140 pounds, while the average model is 5'11" and weighs 117. Her body mass index (BMI) is so low that doctors would consider her dangerously underweight.[35]

And "plus size" isn't even the same. As recently as 2002, plus-size models were typically between the sizes of 12 and 18. By 2012, they range from sizes 6-14. (Model Beverly Johnson was a size 6 at the height of her career. Today she says she probably would have been considered a plus-size model!)[36] To cater to women's desire to be ever skinnier, clothing retailers are even skewing sizes smaller. Today's size 6 was a size

12 on Marilyn Monroe.[37] We can't help feeling lousy about our looks when we're constantly given a standard of thinness that is impossible for most women. As the Young Women's Christian Association pointed out, "Engulfed by a popular culture saturated with images of idealized, airbrushed and unattainable female physical beauty, women and girls cannot escape feeling judged on the basis of their appearance."[38]

So we spend increasing amounts of time and money on improving our looks. As we noted in the first chapter, $10.7 billion is spent annually on cosmetic procedures, and over 92 percent of that is by women.[39] Over the course of a lifetime, the average woman spends almost $450,000 on cosmetic products, treatments, and procedures (according to *Newsweek*).[40] Is this simply trying to look the best we can, or are we judging ourselves as having "flaws" we must correct? Do we devote so much attention to appearance because of our desire to be sex objects? Even if we're uncomfortable with our culture's focus on beauty, we vote to support that culture whenever we buy beauty products. This makes our beauty culture even more dominant.

Have you ever looked in the mirror and thought your looks needed improvement? Maybe you wondered if you'd get a boyfriend if only you had bigger breasts, lost 10 pounds, or had sexier legs. Maybe you felt inadequate compared to models in magazines. (Thanks to Photoshop and retouching, even models don't look like models in magazines!) We're bound to perpetuate this tyranny of beauty unless we step back and see what we're doing to ourselves. We must reconsider the role models we display to girls and young women.

Feminist author Caitlin Moran asks, "Would women fret themselves half to death over how they look or who fancies them if this wasn't the main thing we're still judged on?"[41] It's true that men judge our looks, but perhaps not in the way we assume. Many men actually prefer women who have natural hair and breasts and don't wear heavy makeup. *Women* seem to be the ones who fear the world would end if we all suddenly gave up makeup, breast implants, hair extensions, and Spanx and said, "This is what we really look like. Take it or leave it." We worry that men would back away in horror. Do we really think they'd say, "No more sex for me, thank you"? Most likely, they would adjust. So why are we doing all this primping? Is it for ourselves? Are we competing with other women? Are we doing it to fit in?

Whatever the reason we constantly critique ourselves, we are just as hard on our sisters. Take the beautiful actress Christina Hendricks, the voluptuous siren on the TV series *Mad Men*. People are calling her "fat," simply because she's not a size 0 or 2 like the rest of the women in Hollywood.[42] Who's pressuring her to conform to unrealistic standards and saying she could be a better sex object than she already is? Women! Men don't seem to have a problem with her. Imagine what would happen if women would support each other in doing what's right for each of us as individuals, rather than exerting pressure to conform. Whether it's beauty standards or sexuality, we face the same problems. What unites us is much larger than our differences. We've forgotten the power of sisterhood. And there are other areas where sisterhood is also needed.

Teenage Sexuality: The Powder Keg

Our culture is permeated with sexuality and it affects us all, particularly adolescents. As Ariel Levy says in *Female Chauvinist Pigs: Women and the Rise of Raunch Culture,* "Adolescents are not inventing this culture of exhibitionism and conformity with their own fledgling creative powers. Teens are reflecting back our slobbering culture in miniature."[43] Have you seen the clothing available to preteens these days? Six-year-olds can wear t-shirts and underwear that say

HOT STUFF and EYE CANDY. Teenagers are exposed to the same cultural sexualization that we are as adults. They can't help but be influenced by our overly sexual culture.

"But what does adolescent sexuality have to do with me?" you might ask. Even if you're all grown up, some of these issues may still apply to you. Have you ever given in to a man who didn't want to use a condom because it "decreased his pleasure"? Did you say "no"? Imagine how much harder it would be for a teenager to hold her own.

> Isabelle is a high school sophomore whose mother has already given her "the talk" about disease and pregnancy. Isabelle notices that her mom seems nervous and she tries not to roll her eyes, but she's already heard this stuff in school a zillion times. On the other hand, she would love to know more about the weird feelings her body has been having lately, but she'd be mortified to ask her mom. Isabelle isn't worried about sexually transmitted infections (STIs) or pregnancy since she knows she can use a condom. But she doesn't want a bad reputation at school.
>
> She goes to a party after the football game. There is a lot of beer, and the parents are out of town. As it gets later, couples start hooking up and going off into the bedrooms. A cute guy starts making out with her, which Isabelle enjoys. Eventually he unzips her pants. She starts to stop him, but he tells her how hot she looks and how he's always wanted to hook up with her. Isabelle had wanted to wait a little longer before she had sex, but she doesn't want to disappoint such a cute guy. Plus, the kissing and touching feel great and she is embarrassed to ask him about condoms. Besides, she figures she is the only virgin among her friends so she might as well get it over with!

Perhaps we are so focused on the dangers of sex (or the mechanics of birth control and disease prevention) that we're putting kids at risk by avoiding the discussion of sexual feelings and what to do about them. Experts worry that parents aren't explaining to kids that these sexual feelings are normal, and that having sexual feelings doesn't have to lead to having sex. As Professor Deborah L. Tolman says in her book, *Dilemmas of Desire: Teenage Girls Talk about Sexuality*, "By equating and confounding sexuality with sexual intercourse, we limit how all adolescents learn to conceptualize their romantic relationships and themselves as sexual beings. We also undermine our efforts to educate them and to learn more ourselves about adolescent sexuality through research."[44],*

Although most U.S. public schools have sex education that leans toward abstinence, kids receive many conflicting messages. Why do we expect sex education to be the major influence? Sex education is underfunded and controversial, and an abstinence-only approach simply doesn't work in our oversexed culture. Without information on alternative behaviors, kids are left to their own devices. In a culture filled with sex, polarized by mixed messages, and compounded by peer pressure, it's really no surprise that girls like Isabelle say, "I wasn't planning it. It just happened."

Meanwhile, many parents find it difficult to talk to girls about sexual feelings. They feel unable to overcome the influence of our overly sexualized culture on their child's behavior. Even when parents believe they are having these talks, the kids often don't agree. Is it possible that, even after the women's movement and the sexual revolution, there's still no good way to talk about sex?

According to the Centers for Disease Control, nearly half of American teenagers are sexually active by the tender age of 17. By the age of 19, the numbers rise to over 70 percent.[45] With numbers like these, peer pressure can be a strong influence. Do you remember being young and vulnerable and

*Credit Line: Reprinted by permission of the publisher from DILEMMAS OF DESIRE by Deborah L. Tolman, p. 23, Cambridge, Mass.: Harvard University Press, Copyright © 2002 by the President and Fellows of Harvard College.

picked on for being a little different? They made fun of me for being so tall; they might have made fun of you for wearing glasses. Now they make fun of girls for being virgins. A third of teenage boys report feeling peer pressure to have sex. The majority of teens say waiting to have sex is a nice idea, but nobody really does it.[46]

By now you may be thinking, "Is she preaching abstinence or does she want to pass out condoms in middle school?" But helping teens understand sexuality is too important to approach it so narrowly, as though there are only two perspectives. Society's polarization gives teens mixed messages. It's a recipe for confusion. How can we help our teens if all we do is fight about what we should teach them about sex?

Far too many girls become sexually active too soon for their emotional health. Studies show that girls who experimented with sexual intimacy, even modestly, were more at risk for future depression.[47] It's too soon for us to know if there is a causal link or if girls who are prone to depression are more likely to experiment. Nonetheless, we can't afford to wait another generation to decide to change how we talk to our children about sex.

The proportion of sexually active teens steadily increased from the '50s until the '90s. Since then, teen sexual activity has decreased but remains much higher than it was in the '50s.[48,49] Despite the number of teens having sex, the teen birth rate has been dropping since the late '50s, with the exception of a brief incline between 1988 and 1991.[50] Why the lower birth rates if sexual experience among teens is still so common? According to one study, more teens are both staying abstinent and using birth control.[51]

Among teen moms, more are now single than in years past, reflecting the rising average age that men and women are getting married for the first time (just over 25 for women and 27 for men).[52] While shotgun teen weddings are not ideal, marriage can give a teen more financial stability. With fewer pregnant teens getting married, more young moms are left to support themselves.

Even with this downward trend of teen pregnancies in the United States, our teen birth rate is still *three times* that of any other developed country.[53] By not talking to girls about how to handle their sexual feelings, we may be leaving them more vulnerable and less likely to be prepared for the consequences of sex.

What do European countries do that results in a lower teen birth rate? The biggest difference might be their attitudes toward sex. Esther Perel, therapist and author, says in her book, *Mating in Captivity: Unlocking Erotic Intelligence,* "Europeans, in contrast, view adolescent sexuality as a normal developmental stage on the way to healthy adult sexuality. Sex is not a problem, being irresponsible about sex is."[54] With this view, the key to healthy adolescent sexuality is acting responsibly, like using effective birth control methods and being educated about STIs.

We can learn something from this approach. Right now, our culture is fighting it out: One side says all we need is abstinence. But how can teenagers know how to handle sexual situations if they're not even sure if it's OK to have sexual feelings? The other side supports condoms, birth control pills, and sex education. But sex education generally doesn't teach much about emotions or alternative sexual behaviors. Responsible sex extends to the emotional realm as well.

The solution does not lie at one extreme or the other. Both encouragement to be abstinent and education about safe sex can be appropriate and effective messages, depending on the teen. For many, the most useful conversation will fall somewhere in the middle, including a discussion about alternative behaviors and emotional protection. Here is where the importance of parents comes into play. Research shows that teens who talk more with their parents about sex are less likely to have sex, and those who do are more likely to practice safe sex methods.[55,56] After all, who is better able to decide what values are best for their child than parents? But many parents simply aren't comfortable talking to their kids about sex, whether it's due to societal confusion, individual conflicts, or both.

Somewhere in the Middle

Any talk about sex education and teen sexuality tends to divide people into opposing sides. But it doesn't have to be one extreme or the other. I'm here to talk about the middle ground because that's where most of us live. We know from the past that changing the world only works when we stick together. The division of society stops us from meeting in the middle. The more we fight each other, the farther away we are from creating any real improvement. Instead, we confuse our kids with mixed messages:

- "Value yourself for your mind and personality/ You really need a more flattering bra"

- "Don't sleep around/Make sure you have condoms just in case"

- "Sex is beautiful and natural/Go ask your father"

Ariel Levy again: "But if conservatives are averse to any discussion of sex outside of marriage, liberals often seem allergic to the idea of imposing sexual boundaries or limits… and simply telling kids sex is fine isn't necessarily any more helpful than telling kids sex is bad. Both of these approaches can ultimately have the same result: a silence about the complexities of desire, feminine desire in particular."[57] What's it going to take to openly discuss this issue with our children?

Teen sexuality is complex because everyone is different. Maybe some teens can have responsible sexual relationships that don't lead to disaster, while others just aren't mature enough for sexual intimacy yet. The ideal situation would be parents openly talking with their children about sex—whether they believe in abstinence, safe sex, or something in between—to help them figure out what's right for them.

Unfortunately, this expectation is unrealistic. Many parents are not comfortable talking about sex with their children. We can't assume all parents will have these conversations as often as is needed to make an impact. Sex education may be the only information some teens get. We need to find a bridge between conservatives and liberals. That bridge is respect. We may have opposing political views. But we can respect our differences while working together to make things better for all of us. You might think I'm too optimistic. But one important area where we might be able to begin to find common ground is teaching the young about protecting their hearts.

Is Protecting Your Heart Passé?

Anastasia meets the handsome, mysterious, and tormented billionaire Christian Grey. Although he warns her to "steer clear of him" and says he doesn't "do romance," she's swept up into a confusing relationship involving frightening, secret, and painful sexual practices.[58]

You may recognize this plot line from the best-selling book, *Fifty Shades of Grey*.[59] The popularity of this book shows how we glamorize sex. Whether we intend to or not, we are encouraging people to lead with sex even though the emotional relationship is the prize. Putting sex first often gets you attached before you know what your partner's issues are. This frequently leads to a lot of pain. Are we avoiding something with all this focus on sex? Is it wise to normalize jumping into a sexual relationship with major problems that make it terribly confusing? Some women will think, "If I don't do these things, I'll never find Mr. Right." Although it seemingly worked out for Anastasia and Christian, that was a fairy tale. The red room is not the answer for most people. The more we see movies like this, the more we think protecting your heart is passé.

If our main goal is to be the best sex objects we can be, protecting our hearts is not a priority. Many women today, like Anastasia and then Marnie from earlier in the chapter, feel the only protections they need are condoms and birth control pills, as though protecting your heart is no longer necessary.

In a way, old-fashioned courtship provided some protection for women in a paternalistic society. This is a controversial view, and you might be concerned about my bias. It's hard to tell who is friend or foe on the battlefield of the culture wars of American sexuality. I'm not calling for a return to a previous culture. The strict expectation of premarital virginity restricted how open we could be about our sexuality, but it also protected us. At least in the 1950s, courtship gave many women time to figure out what kind of man he was before agreeing to marry him. The courtship process meant women weren't as likely to have their emotions muddled by sex unless they knew the man very well. They didn't need the phrase, "he's just not that into you." Courtship took care of that. There was some emotional distance without sex to get women attached. They could find out whether a man was a good guy before they gave him their hearts. Courtship supported the idea that slow can be sexy.

Because premarital sex was "forbidden," women had limited options. But they did have social support for saying "no." In today's highly sexual culture, it's harder to say "no," or "let's wait," or "when I get to know you better." Of course, the punishments for breaking the rule of premarital virginity were much worse than the stigma of being a virgin today. Still, it's a problem when kids get teased for being virgins and women don't feel supported by our culture to say "no."

I'm not saying we should return to an era of fewer options. Options are great—when they are truly options and not expectations. Let's take an example. It used to be that a woman should not ride a bicycle because it was immodest (remember, we had to ride sidesaddle on a horse too!). Today in the United States, no one thinks twice about a woman riding a bike. But you probably should wear a helmet, right? I'm not suggesting that women be stopped from riding bikes, only that they consider taking safety precautions.

Yes, some people will think you're uncool if you wear a helmet. Others will applaud your common sense. The argument for bike helmets creates controversy, just as my stance on casual sex does. But society doesn't shame us for protecting our heads. We all want the freedom to make mistakes, even if they can harm us. This isn't a perfect analogy because, obviously, ALL skulls need protection. Each of us must decide if we need to protect our individual hearts (and skulls) and how to do so, preferably without public shaming.

Many of you may think protections for women infantilize us, as if to suggest we aren't able to figure out what is best for us and need societal norms to help us. Some women even think I want to return us to aspects of the patriarchal society of the past. Again, I'm in the middle, between severe restrictions and "anything goes." I'm advocating for societal guidelines, not rules that can't be broken. Many women will be fine without these suggestions because they are already their own Brands of Sexy. I'm not saying we should take away any of their freedoms. But, for those who are still struggling to find their way, some basic dating principles encouraged by their sisters would provide a base for each woman to build upon as she finds her own standards in dating and sexuality. We need support, not restriction.

In the past, gentlemen were supposed to take care of ladies. This was a form of protection. Although, in many cases, it was controlling and paternalistic. Today, some say providing for a partner and family is rewarding for men and that we are rejecting men with our belief that we can do it all on our own. We can pump our own gas, support ourselves financially, and even have babies without them, as though we are saying that men are not necessary. Are we pushing away our potential protectors? In our grandmothers' day, men who "got around" were scoundrels. They were shunned by respectable young ladies. Now, even the most together, intelligent, professional women fall for bad boys. Some find nice guys too boring.

Do we simply not expect as much from men anymore? Women are more likely to finish high school, go to college, and graduate from college than men.[60,61] Maybe we no longer want paternalistic protection, but do we really want to give up on expecting men to live up to any kind of standards of behavior? Hanna Rosin says in *The End of Men: And the Rise of Women*, "...the rise of women is associated with the slow erosion of marriage and even a growing cynicism about love."[62]

We have more power now—men no longer protect us, and we have power through education, social position, financial independence, and mobility. But the flip side is that we're alone with the responsibility of shielding ourselves from pregnancy, STIs, heartbreak, or just being taken for granted. Sure, we want options, and we don't want to be passive. But simply being "modern" doesn't give us power. Power comes from realizing that we always have a choice and doing what's best for us as individuals. Even if these old protections seem outdated and unnecessary, without them we are vulnerable to being hurt. Excellent instincts and intuition can help us find our way in this unfamiliar territory and lower the chances of heartache.

Making the right choices for you puts you on the path to getting what you want. Making wrong choices sends you down a costly detour, filled with delay, heartbreak, and possibly not reaching your goals at all. Even if you do reach your goals eventually, and you can tolerate the emotional pain of poor choices along the way, it still takes longer to get there. Thinking through what is best for you at each step of the way creates a much more direct, and enjoyable, route to get where you want to be.

So What Now?

In the past, being "normal" meant living through your husband and kids. Now, we feel pressure to look amazing, to have spectacularly impressive careers, and to have sex at least three times a week (since everyone else is, right?). Trying to fit in with what we think is "normal" restricts our individuality as much as it did in the '50s but in ways that look so different that it's easy for us to completely overlook it. Fitting someone else's vision of a "modern woman" may not work for you, but are you trying to squeeze into it anyway, like a pair of jeans that don't fit?

Consider the following paradox: We need confidence to resist cultural or individual pressures, but the process of resisting improves our confidence. When you pretend to be confident, others often treat you with more respect. Once you see you can do it, it can transform your life.

As trailblazers who are struggling to figure out what works best for us in a rapidly changing world, we've had to get tough. Many of us have adapted by adopting a masculine vision of success—high-level careers and casual sex to keep relationship demands to a minimum. This pattern works for many women, but at what cost? Many are becoming worka-holics, like the fathers they grew up with. Others are choosing to raise children alone. Are we transforming the world into a kinder, gentler place, or have we just become more aggressive to compete in the workplace and with each other?

Society is waking up to the reality of trying to have it all today. Anne-Marie Slaughter, who is an author, president of the New America Foundation, and Bert G. Kerstetter '66 University Professor Emerita of Politics and International Affairs at Princeton University, says in *The Atlantic*, "I still strongly believe that women can 'have it all' (and that men can too). I believe that we can 'have it all at the same time,' but not today, not with the way America's economy and society are currently structured."[63]

Redefining what it means to be sexy, feminine, power-ful women is important so we can express our individuality rather than strive for an ideal which is unattainable for many, if not most. Knowledge is power. Now that we understand how we got here, let's look at what is needed to develop our own Brand of Sexy. Remember, being your own Brand of Sexy means figuring out what you want, what works for you as an individual, and what strategies will help you reach your goals. In other words:

1. You always have a choice.

2. Media and peer pressure solutions might not be right for you.

3. Slow can be sexy.

4. Your voice matters.

5. If a guy isn't respecting your voice, move on.

As you read on, remember the importance of sisterhood. Ideally, women wouldn't need to please others to figure out what is right for them, but many do. Research has shown that, if we feel our behavior is going to be evaluated by other people, we are more likely to do what is culturally expected.[64] So, when the expectation is to be highly sexual, women can feel pressured into behaving this way. Sisterhood can help us to stand up to these expectations. Feeling supported by our sisters could help us feel more comfortable doing what's right for us as individuals. If we had support from women in being our own Brands of Sexy, we might feel safer if we gained a few pounds or had pimples, wrinkles, or other imperfections. It might be easier to decide how to handle dating and sexual decisions if we expected acceptance rather than criticism and shame. Together, we could create a consistent direction for young adults, rather than confusing them with mixed messages. Imagine if women had mentors rather than critics who constantly disagree.

In the next sections, we'll take a step-by-step approach to navigating this brand new world:

- How to know where you're going (Chapter 3)

- How we're built (Chapter 4)

- How to protect our hearts (Chapter 5)

- The importance of emotional hygiene (Chapter 6)

- The Single Woman's 12-Piece Dating Toolbox (Chapter 7)

By Chapter 8, you'll be ready for a trial run of all the new ideas you've learned, with a quiz to see where you are in this process. Are you ready to be your own Brand of Sexy?

For more information on the issues discussed in this chapter, including teenage sexuality, please visit my website at www.beyourownbrandofsexy.com.

3

Know Where You're Going

*"If you don't know where you're going,
you might end up somewhere else."*
—Yogi Berra

A s she struggled with weight, cigarettes, and alcohol; coped with a commitment-phobic womanizer; and listened to "smug marrieds" tell her to hurry to find a man, "Singleton" Bridget Jones stole our hearts.[65] Helen Fielding's wildly popular book and movie about modern single life validated our struggles, made us laugh at our heartbreak, and helped us see we weren't alone. Bridget is every modern woman, trying to live up to everybody's expectations, and frequently falling short.

Single life feels like going to a casino for the very first time. Everybody has a different opinion about which game is best and what strategies work. It can be overwhelming and confusing to figure out which game to play and how to play it. The stakes are high, and there's a lot to lose. Do we want Mr. Right? Or Mr. Right Now? (Or Mr. So-Far-So-Good?) Do we play hard to get, or should we be "modern women" and date like men?

Julia has started dating Kyle, a handsome, successful sales manager. She finds him very attractive and enjoys their conversations. He seems interested, but he usually calls her for dates at the last minute, which rubs her the wrong way. She tells herself he's probably just really busy and it's hard to plan in advance. She accepts the dates and then feels slightly resentful. Julia considers telling Kyle she's busy when he calls so late. One friend says, "You're a modern woman. You don't have to play games like that." But another friend says, "Maybe the last-minute thing is a sign he's just not that into you." At the same time, her sister warns her not to drive away a great guy by being too demanding.

Nobody can say women don't have a lot of choices anymore! But it certainly makes it harder to figure out which option is best. We lost the old-fashioned dating rules but didn't replace them with a new set. Society gives us mixed messages about what it means to be "modern." The expectations of our friends and families aren't crystal clear either. We're told we should focus on our independence and education or career: "You're too young to get serious about anyone." "How will you support yourself if you get divorced?" But we also hear, "How's your love life?" "Do you have a boyfriend?" "I can't believe you aren't married yet!" Remember, our friends and families are also pioneers in this era fraught with change and confusion, so they may not realize how mixed-up their messages are.

Our emotions can run the gamut when we feel we don't live up to those expectations. Some of us feel inadequate. Others feel resentful or angry at the criticism or pressure. Or maybe we just feel alone and sad because our friends and families don't understand what we're going through. The more emotional we get, the more confusing it can become.

Sometimes these expectations make it harder to figure out our priorities. How much time do I have for a relationship if my main focus is school or a career? Is it easier to just have casual relationships because they take up less time? If I have a boyfriend, won't that cut down my time for me? Without a roadmap, we have lots of choices but much less clarity about which path to choose.

Is More Better?

Our society loves having lots of choices. Being single and childless no longer makes you a "frumpy old maid" like it did in the past. Now you can be seen as worldly, glamorous, or sophisticated. But "having it all" can sometimes include confusion and inadequacy, if you have too many choices.

Barry Schwartz's book, *The Paradox of Choice: Why More Is Less*, suggests that too many options lead to higher expectations and more opportunity for disappointment, regret, self-blame, and trouble making decisions.[66] As an example, he thought it would be simple to buy some jeans. But he is overwhelmed by all the options, from basic Levi's to $400 designer jeans. We can relate. We buy a pair and like how we look in them, but sometimes we have the nagging feeling that we might have missed an even better choice.

How does this relate to dating? Schwartz points out that men and women are waiting five more years to marry than they did a generation ago. He says that "whereas delaying marriage . . . would seem to promote self-discovery, this freedom and self-exploration seems to leave many people feeling more lost than found."[67] Is it harder to commit when we have too many options (so many men, so little time)? Sure, this guy is great, but what if I miss out on someone better?

Today many young women think that it is best to have the freedom to enjoy active sex lives without the commitment that might interfere with academic or professional goals. But some disagree. Susan Patton, Princeton class president of

53

1977 and author of *Marry Smart: Advice for Finding THE ONE*, told women in *The Daily Princetonian* that their future happiness depended on the man they married, and their time at Princeton was their best opportunity to find a suitable partner.[68] Writer Julia Shaw pointed out in *Slate* that she and her husband grew up together in their marriage rather than marrying after they grew up.[69]

Modern women are delighted to have choices because we know how limited our options were in the past. The strict codes of behavior restricted women much more than men. Because things have changed, we don't have to wait for a man to call anymore. We don't have to be passive! We can ask him out if we like him. Many of us tried it out just to show that we could. Some of us like doing things that way, but others aren't comfortable with it. The hard part is how to decide what's best for us, especially with the mixed messages coming from these two camps. "Asking him out gives you power." "No, we have to play hard to get." Are you confused yet?

We also wonder whether we should treat men differently now that we are equals. Should we go Dutch if we can afford it? Is it OK to want him to pay? Some women feel guilty if they prefer the man to pay, so they offer, secretly hoping he'll refuse. Meanwhile, he goes along with her idea, thinking paying is what she wants, leaving her disappointed. Other women feel paying prevents men from assuming that, if they buy us dinner, we're supposed to be "dessert." And, as much as we want to be treated as equals, we can't forget the fact that women still make 77 percent of what men earn, so we're not on a level playing field.[70]

Men are also confronted with too many choices now that there are no clear dating rules. Should he offer to pay for every date? Most dates? Does it depend on how much each person makes? When a woman offers to pay, does she expect him to turn her down or does she mean it? Will he offend a woman if he opens a door for her, or does that depend on how old she is or where she grew up?

Herd Mentality

Whether we're conforming to cultural norms, caving to peer pressure, or imitating a trend because it seems like a good idea, we don't even realize how much other people influence us. The larger the trend, the more influential it becomes because it seems like extra proof that something big is happening.

James Surowiecki claims, counterintuitively, in his best-selling book, *The Wisdom of Crowds*, that, although we trust experts and distrust the decisions of the masses, crowds make the better decisions.[71] If there is a free exchange of competing ideas, crowds do better than experts with choices ranging from companies making investments to answers on game shows. The caveat is that the decision makers must make these decisions *free from the influence of others*. If each person in a game show audience makes a guess, the majority rule will likely be more accurate than a single expert's guess. But, if the audience members work together and agree upon one group guess, the expert is more likely to be accurate. The difference here comes down to whether a person makes a decision on her own or is influenced by others.

Surowiecki says, "If people just keep following the lead of others, regardless of what happens, the well-being of the group suffers."[72] The more we try to make our attitudes about sex conform to what we think everyone else is doing, the more confused about sex we will be. And when we try to make ourselves act like everyone else, we have even bigger problems, ranging from broken dates to broken hearts. But the more conscious we are of societal pressure, the more power we have. Being aware of these outside influences helps free us from their spell.

Sex Is All Around

As we saw in Chapter 1, sexual images are all over our culture. Sex sells, and we're constantly bombarded by images that objectify women. This gives us the message that our value comes from our sexual appeal and behavior. The more exposed we are to these images, the more desensitized we become. That makes it harder to draw the line between wanting to look our best and thinking, "If I don't look sexy, there's something wrong with me." Meanwhile, teen girls are developing eating disorders in epic proportions, and plastic surgery rates are skyrocketing—for women and men.[73,74]

This sexual saturation is even confusing for men. Men may not be objectified as constantly as we are, but they face pressures too, including feeling judged on their success, their wealth, and their virility. Because men are expected to be single-mindedly focused on sex, some refer to this performance pressure as "booty duty." Other men worry that they'll be considered gay if they're not aggressive enough or if they turn down sex.

And lately media images increasingly sexualize younger and younger girls, in fashion, advertising, even kiddie beauty pageants. We don't have much research on how media objectification affects adults, but we do know it's very damaging to young girls. The American Psychological Association issued strong warnings about how harmful these sexual images are to girls' self-image and development.[75]

So parents are confused. They want to keep their daughters innocent young girls without making them feel totally out of touch with popular culture. Is a mom being overprotective if she forbids revealing clothing or recommends abstinence? (Especially when the daughter says, "Everyone else is doing it"—and the daughter feels like she is telling the truth!)

Anthropologist David Murray said, "Our culture is to a large extent experimenting with eroticizing the child."[76] Despite the warnings, we are shocked when we are faced with the overt sexuality of increasingly younger girls.

What's a Girl Supposed to Do?

So what happens when those girls grow up? Do these issues suddenly get clearer? Or do we just begin to accept the need to look and be sexy? Remember, I'm not pushing total abstinence or condoms in preschool—I'm in the middle ground, where most of us live. But, in our confusion, we often mold ourselves into whatever we perceive "normal" to be, whether it works for us or not. Here's how this plays out for the single woman: "When's the right time to have sex?" "Is the first date too soon?" "Will he lose interest if I wait too long?" "Will he still respect me in the morning?" "I'm a modern woman. Shouldn't I be able to have sex 'like a man'?" "Why do I seem to get attached when I do?" "Will it ruin my reputation?" "I knew it was just a hookup, so why does it bother me that he didn't call?" and "How am I supposed to find time to answer all these questions anyhow?" (Don't worry, that's what this book is for!)

The problem with being confused and trying to be "normal" is that your version of "normal" depends on the situation. Normal can be vastly different, depending on if you're hanging with the girls at a club or a business lunch, or having tea with your mother. In a culture of mixed messages, molding ourselves into normalcy is certain to be very confusing. And when our cultural standard of "normalcy" is so often tinged with an air of sexuality, it's no wonder that girls become women who have difficulty knowing what is best for them.

With sex oozing from every magazine and TV in America, we quickly learn how important it is. We read stories that tell us how good sex is for your health, but nobody talks about the fact that women regret having casual sex more than men do.[77] Perhaps this is related to our double standard (men are praised for their sexual behavior, while women are judged to be promiscuous), but that's no reason to ignore it as an important consideration. Does casual sex simply not work for some of us?

The women's movement and the sexual revolution didn't bury the double standard and didn't change the way we're "built." Knowing what's socially acceptable doesn't necessarily change the way we feel, but we seem to think it should. "Normal behavior" comes in a number of flavors—abstinence only, have sex "like a man," monogamy is old fashioned, and many others. Seeking social acceptance has the potential to make us feel bad about the way we feel, leading to even more confusion.

> Andrea is getting ready for her fourth date with Amir, a great guy she hasn't slept with yet. She finds him very attractive, and Amir has made it clear he'd like to go further. So would she, but she wants to do what's best for the relationship. Andrea worries that Amir will lose patience if she holds off too much longer. But she's also worried that he'll be like guys she has dated in the past who backed off once sex entered the picture and the thrill of the chase was gone. Her friends are delighted she's found such a great guy. Some are encouraging her to stop stalling and "seal the deal," while some tell her to hold out for a commitment, since "men don't buy the cow when they get the milk for free." (Believe it or not, people still say that!) Andrea likes Amir a lot, but all the different advice is confusing. And he's such a great kisser that she's afraid she won't think clearly if they start making out!

Self-Help

We're trying to figure out what's normal so we can transform ourselves. But guess where else we get mixed messages from about what's "normal"? Self-help books! Bridget Jones thinks her friend Jude "must stop beating herself over the head" with one self-help book and see her situation with "Vile Richard" from the perspective of a different self-help book.[78] How do you know which author has the right advice for your situation? Left to our own devices, even these potentially helpful guides can cause more confusion.

If you tend to be easily influenced by others' opinions, it is likely that conflicting advice from different self-help books will confuse you even more. All books are biased—and the one you're reading is no exception. The only difference is that I don't pretend to know exactly what's best for you. I mean, I haven't even met you! But I can give you some things to think about to help you decide what actually *is* best for you.

We're all different, so using self-help methods requires you to be as objective about yourself as possible—and we all know how impossible that is. Isn't that one of the reasons we talk to our friends, participate in online conversations, or seek psychotherapy? We need a more objective opinion because we too often second-guess whether what we're doing or thinking is in our own best interest. Or sometimes we are wrong when we think we are doing what's best for us.

Like for Bridget's friend Jude, sometimes self-help books just make us feel worse about ourselves, but the answer isn't just to find another book recommending a different strategy. Before we can benefit from anyone else's advice and perspective, you need to know what works for you.

What Do *You* Want?

Trying to live up to others' expectations can be OK, but it can also backfire. If you can easily meet another person's expectations, then you can both be happy. If their expectations are too high, confusing, or just different than what you want, it's a problem. (And how many people want exactly what you want? If you've ever had to return a gift thinking, "Why did she pick that?" you know how hard it is even for your friends to know what works for you.) Consider what happens if you can never please a parent growing up. That situation can lead to a chronic desire to please others, like you're reliving the experience of trying to please and always falling short. Trying to figure out what you want then becomes especially tricky because it's overshadowed by a need to please. And women tend to be real people-pleasers.

Surprise! People-pleasing doesn't always work for women. Our needs won't be met if we're ignoring what we want. This tendency can make it harder to figure out if the guy you're dating is a nice guy. If you simply want to please him, you might miss the cues that tell you whether he'll be any good at pleasing you. For instance, women are more satisfied in their relationships when their partners make an effort to understand their negative feelings, even if these men aren't accurate in their understanding.[79] But, if we don't admit when we are unhappy, we don't give men the opportunity to show us if they are willing to try to understand how we feel. In this way, our negative feelings can be our ally and can illuminate valuable information about a man's character.

Sometimes you just have to do what's best for you, whether others like it or not. Now please don't take this as an invitation to do whatever you want without regard to the consequences or the risks. But, unless you do what's ultimately best for you, you can end up tying yourself in knots trying to please others. Remember, this is what is meant by being your own Brand of Sexy—doing what's best for you emotionally, not doing something just to please a guy, your friends, or a self-help book, or just because everyone else is doing it. Nobody's saying this is easy.

So how do you clarify any confusion you might have? How do you begin to be your own Brand of Sexy? Think about what's important to you in your life. What are your priorities? Is career very important? Education? Are you planning on having children? Is having a good relationship one of your goals? Marriage? Do you want all of these? What are your priorities for now? Do you want to focus on career, with lots of time before your clock starts ticking? Maybe you aren't ready for a serious relationship but want to learn how to screen out guys who aren't that into you. Or maybe you just want to have casual dating and sexual experiences. Here's where my bias comes in. I believe that women who choose to have casual sexual experiences should consider the possibility that they might need to protect their hearts.

At-Home Exercises: What Would *You* Do?

For decades, researchers told us that women are people-pleasers because of cultural programming.[80] Since the women's movement, many of us believe that's no longer true about women. Sure, you're a modern woman, with more power than the women in the '60s, so perhaps you don't think this applies to you. But consider this experiment. Close your eyes and imagine yourself in the following scenarios. How do you feel? What do you think? How do you act? Write your answers someplace private so you can go back to them later to look for any patterns from which you can learn.

Scenario 1: Ben asks you to dinner and you have a great time until the check comes and he tells you he forgot his wallet at home. Are you disappointed? Annoyed? Do you think you should pay because you're a modern woman? Or perhaps you think, "Oh, well, I can afford it. Men don't always have to pay. I'm a modern woman." Or, "I don't want him to get mad at me." Or, "He's so cute, he probably has tons of women happy to pay for their dates with him."

Scenario 2: You met Tom, an interesting guy, at a business event. He asked for your number and called you a few days later to ask you out. However, he says he lives an hour's drive away and asks if you can meet him halfway so his drive isn't so long. Some of your friends tell you, "That's only fair," and some say he should come pick you up for the first date. How do you feel?

Scenario 3: You chat with Wyatt, a cute guy, at a party. You feel the chemistry with him right away, but he never asks for your number. Do you offer it to him anyway? Or ask for his number? Or do you think that would be a mistake (since you just saw the movie *He's Just Not That Into You*)? Do you quickly text a friend for advice?

Now think about these situations with a twist (and note your responses to these suggestions):

Scenario 1 Revisited: When Ben tells you he left his wallet at home, would you be comfortable saying, "Did I misunderstand? I thought you'd invited me, so I didn't bring my wallet, just my ID"? Would that make you feel good about yourself, worried about his reaction, or wonder what your friends would think? And what if he seems upset? Would you suddenly "find" some cash in your purse?

Scenario 2 Revisited: When Tom asks you to meet him halfway, you say, "I'd love to get together *sometime*, but that won't work for me." Does this feel like taking care of your needs? Do you wonder if it sounds too old-fashioned? Or are you worried you're making it too hard for him and he might lose interest? Are you worried about what your girlfriends would advise?

Scenario 3 Revisited: If you didn't give Wyatt your number or ask for his, do you regret it after the party? Did you make excuses for him in your mind ("He's shy" or "He's just waiting for me to make the first move")? In other situations where you've given a guy your number before he asked, did he end up calling? Is he more likely to take you for granted or to be looking for casual sex than a guy who asks for your number?

What Do You Think?

How did you feel about your reactions to these stories? Perhaps they reminded you of some of your own experiences or reinforced your confusion about dating. Have you ever talked yourself into doing something that made you uncomfortable or that wasn't what you really wanted? How about Julia, the woman at the beginning of this chapter, who vacillates between making excuses for Kyle's last-minute dates and standing up for herself? Is she being modern or talking herself out of what she wants? Being aware of what we tell ourselves in those situations is the first step in an ongoing process of finding your own Brand of Sexy.

Save your answers so you can look for patterns as you go through the stories in the coming chapters. Notice the behaviors that are not working for you. By repeating these tendencies, you may be sabotaging your own happiness.

If you are feeling even more confused, you are not alone. I've raised a lot of complex questions. I'm not here to tell you what to do, but I can help you think through these issues. As you get a better understanding of the modern dating world, you can identify what is getting in your way.

Teasing out societal influences is an important first step. How can we be our own Brand of Sexy if we're restricted by society? Pressures can play out in a number of ways, such as worrying about what your friends would say, being nervous that a guy might be upset, or feeling confused about what to do in various situations. Of course, we're more likely to be influenced by society if we have personal issues as well. Our baggage becomes much clearer and easier to address if we untangle the influence of our culture. The more clarity we have about our issues, the less society is able to sway our choices. And how concerned do we really have to be about our friends disagreeing with our ideas about how to handle these situations with guys? We're the ones who have to deal with the aftermath of our decisions. The more we worry about our friends' disapproval, the more likely we are to have big problems with figuring out whose advice to take, especially when they all have different opinions. If you want a relationship where your feelings matter, don't let anyone talk you out of those feelings.

You've completed the first step of looking at what you want for yourself and teasing out how society may be influencing your choices. Even if you don't know exactly what you want, you probably have some ideas of what you don't want. That's a great start. In future chapters, we'll continue to get more clarity. In some ways, step one is the hardest because we don't always recognize how we are influenced by others. It's a whole new way of looking at the world.

In the next chapter we'll explore what psychiatrists, psychologists, scientists, and a noted anthropologist have to say about how we're "built." (Yes, there will be some science but no lab work or chemistry formulas, I promise. Just some fascinating insights and surprising information!)

4

Consider How We're "Built"

"Men are from Earth.
Women are from Earth. Deal with it."
—George Carlin

Let's enter another realm where experts give conflicting opinions—science. The quotes around "built" suggest this supposed hardwiring is not written in stone, the way it sounds. We want to know why we do what we do. Human brains crave simple explanations. But here's a news flash—we're not that simple, especially when it comes to the differences between the sexes. We're not simply hardwired like computers. Our brains make us intricately more complicated.

Generalities are a good starting point, so let's begin with the ones that are useful. Keep in mind that this doesn't mean you have to exactly fit into a category or that you're a freak if you don't. There are scientists who insist that biology primarily controls how we behave. Other, equally respected scientists claim that our culture and how we are raised are much stronger influences than biology.

But, as we have seen earlier, one size in biology or psychology does not fit all. It's important to understand how both biology and culture affect us, but to also understand that we don't have all the answers. When it comes to romance and sexuality, human beings are diverse and complex. Some women want men who can provide for them, while others prefer to be the breadwinners. Some men prefer women with hourglass figures, and others don't. There are men and women who are straight, gay, bisexual, and transgender. While some generalizations apply to some or most of us, each of us remains unique.

For generations, it was a given: Men and women are different. Gender determined how people were treated and how they were expected to behave. The women's movement caused us to question that ancient belief. After all, if we're equal, how different can we be? In the past, women were put down for being "the weaker sex," both physically and emotionally. This made us vulnerable to exploitation and control. Women were sick of hearing "truths," such as "Women can never hold a responsible position such as President because they are too emotional." People used these beliefs to justify why we weren't as successful as men in the workplace.

On the other hand, these days we often hear it said that there are *no* differences between the two sexes. But let's be realistic—it's obvious how different men and women look, reflecting different hormonal influences that affect our bodies. We have different physical structures, which on average does mean that men are physically stronger.[81] Those hormones affect our brains differently too. Generally speaking, there are psychological and emotional differences between men and women.[82] But none of these facts make us "weaker."

Today a lot of women don't want to acknowledge that we are different from men. We fear that recognizing this will return us to a society that used this fact to discriminate against us. But the problem with the past was never that women were different. It was that we were treated as though we were inferior. We can still be equal and yet acknowledge our important differences.

Today we don't know if equality means there are no differences between us. Science to the rescue!

Don't Believe Everything You Read

We love reading articles with an evolutionary psychology slant. You know, the ones where they tell you men are programmed to want sex, and women want to marry men with money. They tell us our ancestors were more likely to survive to produce *us* because they acted on these desires. So we can't help feeling this way too. Following every article in print makes for good conversation but can mislead you about human nature. Sure, some of these writers have interesting theories. But many have criticized their data, saying their science is weak. For example, research conducted with college-educated women found that women want men with money.[83] But they didn't test women from lower socioeconomic levels. Perhaps the women they studied were just looking for guys with backgrounds similar to their own. These results don't necessarily apply to all women. We like to read these types of studies because we're curious about what makes us tick. Plus, it's reassuring to be told that we behave the way we do because of how we're built—"We can't help it!" But not all scientists agree. Does anyone have the answers?

The behavioral ecologists disagree. They say that we're better off (more "evolutionarily fit") if we can adapt to change in our environment. So they disagree with the evolutionary psychologists, who say men want women with hourglass figures (smaller waist + big hips = more fertile) and women want men who are good providers. In the Stone Age, this meant a caveman who brings home the most meat; these days, it's a Wall Street broker with good taste in jewelry. Recent research says that these preferences are only true in countries where women depend on men financially.[84] And, according to this research, the more financially independent women become, the more likely we are to pick a man based on his looks instead of his money. (Wait, does this mean we never notice emotional qualities? Are they saying we never look past nice hair and six-pack abs?)

How ironic. We hate generalizations and stereotyping when we're labeled in a negative way ("Women are too emotional"), but they're not so bad if they let us off the hook ("I can't help it. It's my genetic makeup"). The moral here is to take everything you read with a grain of salt, especially if all those stereotypes cause you to be harder on yourself. Take Lisa, who read that men are hardwired to prefer hourglass figures. She is now convinced that, if she doesn't have a curvy figure, she's biologically bound to become a spinster who talks to her cats. Lisa wrongly believes that "biology is destiny," not that biology influences some things but we make our own futures.

To make matters worse, the media often presents science articles sensationally. But they aren't always accurate. Take the 1997 article that was suddenly reported in 2009 as "Regular Sex Improves Health and Doubles Life Expectancy."[85] This study was criticized because it was not clear whether sex improved longevity or whether people who were healthier were able to have more sex.[86] And guess how many women were in the study? None! But most people didn't remember the critique, only the questionable longevity message.

Let's briefly talk about how to figure out if you should believe a study or not. Ideally, the people being studied represent the general population. If only a specific group is studied (like men, in the example above), the results can't be applied to everyone (men and women). Paying attention to how the study is set up is also important. In some, researchers compare two groups of people (one group that takes a medication and another that takes a placebo pill, for example). These results are usually more reliable than if they only observe one group (everyone takes the medication). Relying on people to report their behavior can be problematic because they may not always be honest. For example, men tend to inflate how many women they have slept with. Women tend to bend the truth in the other direction.[87] This can lead to inaccurate results. It is important to be critical of scientific studies, particularly when the results are dramatic and receive a lot of attention in the media.

Are We From Different Planets?

It's easier to sell books when the author makes the concepts easy to understand and the conclusions sensational. The danger in simplifying complex scientific ideas is that readers might misunderstand and miss the nuances. This can lead us to believe we're programmed like computers to be who we are. It's just not that simple.

Deborah Tannen, author of *You Just Don't Understand: Women and Men in Conversation*, showed us how we're speaking different languages.[88] John Gray, author of *Men Are From Mars, Women Are From Venus: A Practical Guide for Improving Communication and Getting What You Want in Your Relationships*, told us men and women are from different planets.[89] They've helped us bridge communication gaps and have more empathy for the opposite sex. Oxford Language Professor Deborah Cameron, author of *The Myth of Mars and Venus: Do Men and Women Really Speak Different Languages?*, says it's true that we don't communicate in the same ways.[90] But she says, "The folk-belief that women talk more than men persists because it provides a justification for an ingrained social prejudice."[91] Cameron points out that evolutionary psychology projects our current prejudices back to prehistory and turns them into "timeless truths about the human condition."[92] This just reinforces those prejudices.

In *The Female Brain*[93] and *The Male Brain*,[94] Louann Brizendine says hardwired differences exist although we fear prejudice from them. These views stirred so much controversy that some accused her of weak science and stereotyping.[95] She now says, "As modern society continues its evolutionary process, we'll always discuss the line where biology, anthropology and our high-minded selves push and pull each other toward the direction we want to go."[96]

Pink Brain, Blue Brain: How Small Differences Can Grow Into Troublesome Gaps—And What We Can Do About It author Lise Eliot says that the focus on hardwiring has oversimplified a complex story.[97] Our brains are also influenced by our upbringing. She agrees there are gender differences but says we're not really from different planets. It's more like "men are from North Dakota, women are from South Dakota."[98] She thinks "nurture" is just as important as "nature."[99] And the more we believe the hardwiring camp, the more likely we are to perpetuate the differences between the sexes.

Eliot says that we assume boys and girls are hardwired to behave differently. So parents unknowingly reinforce those stereotypes. We think "boys are more immature" and "girls are more verbal." But most of these differences are actually a result of early socialization, rather than hardwiring. We encourage certain traits in girls and others in boys. Eliot says: "By appreciating how sex differences emerge—rather than assuming them to be fixed biological facts—we can help all children reach their fullest potential, close the troubling gaps between boys and girls, and ultimately end the gender wars that currently divide us."[100]

Which side is right? Maybe neither. Everybody's different. Hardwiring is just too simple to explain our complexity. We have different parents, giving us different messages, and different cultures which shape us. So maybe *some* women want men with lots of money, and others just want compatible, loving partners. *Some* men are "players," and others are nice guys who don't stray because they care about their partners' feelings. You don't have to force yourself into a box where you don't belong, or put all men into the same box either. Read the books, they have a lot of interesting ideas, but take what they say with a grain of salt and don't let them discourage you.

OK, OK, there are good points made by both sides. Yes, as evolutionary psychologists point out, biological differences affect us, and yes, behavioral ecologists give us important information about the way our culture affects us. But the truth is likely somewhere in the middle. Do we need to know whether it's culture vs. hardwiring, nature vs. nurture? No! Do we want to get into the middle of a "battle of the scientists"? No! We just want to know what works for us, right? (In case you do want to learn more, there are references and related books and articles listed at the end of this book.)

So it's time to wipe the slate clean, as though we have no preconceived notions on this subject, as if you haven't read every book and article that told you how you're hardwired. Let's get into the basics of what women want.

What *Do* Women Want?

Guess who's willing to spend lots of money researching women's sexual desire? Drug companies. They would love to find the "female Viagra" that represents a so-far-elusive gold mine to them. "Estimates" say 40 percent of women have low sexual desire.[101] It's not easy to fix because what drives women's desire is complex. Our conflicted culture tells us both sex is shameful and you should be having lots of it. Add the pressures on women to "have it all"—and we're too exhausted for sex. And our sexual partners might expect lots of sex (because it seems like that is the norm).

In their pursuit of understanding women's sex drive, sex researchers have discovered that it's extremely difficult to separate cultural and biological factors. They think sexual desire is complicated, idiosyncratic, and more dependent on situational factors.[102] After all, many women have difficulty asking for what they want. And their partners can't read their minds about what turns them on. Also, women often focus on everyone else's needs instead of their own. This makes it hard to fully embrace the pleasure involved. In fact, when they studied women's sexual arousal, they discovered that women often can't tell when they are sexually aroused, even when their bodies show signs of it.[103]

Researchers theorize that, for women, being desired sparks lust.[104] Women have lower sex drives than men.[105] Within long-term relationships women are much more likely to lose their interest in sex.[106] Women need more of a trigger to get turned on.[107] Researchers wonder whether the being-desired stimulus weakens over time in a relationship.[108] Maybe their partner is slightly less interested. Or maybe the woman feels her partner is trapped, as though he's no longer making a choice to be with her. Dr. Marta Meana, Professor of Psychology at University of Nevada at Las Vegas, says, "What women want is a real dilemma—women want male partners that are strong and virile but also sensitive and caring. Getting the right calibration of these often opposing characteristics can be a challenge."[109]

No wonder women are a mystery to men. And drug companies have yet to be able to bottle this magic potion. But it's confusing for us too. What should you learn from Dr. Meana's research? It's important for you to figure out what kind of desire and caring you want and what it will look and feel like. We want to be desired. So, when a man wants us, it can be tempting to get sexually involved. But if we want desire *and* caring, sex without commitment puts us at risk. Hookups can be inherently disappointing, unless you want only to satisfy your lust and want only to be sexually desired. If he desires you but only wants casual sex, his desire might not last very long. Casual relationships only satisfy a relatively short-term type of desire.

Lots of choice also means more chance of regret. When it comes to dating, men are more likely to regret paths not chosen ("If only I had asked her out"). But women are more likely to regret things they have done ("If only I hadn't slept with him").[110] Men can regret casual sex too, but evolutionary psychologists say the regret for women is due to the responsibilities of pregnancy and childbirth.[111] But the double standard is alive and well and may influence these feelings too. We worry about our reputations, while men are supposed to gain sexual experience at almost any cost.

Although we're more oriented toward relationships,[112] many of us feel ambivalent about sex. Who wouldn't be ambivalent with pregnancy, double standards, and broken hearts to burden us? Meanwhile, many single women are likely to agree with biological anthropologist Dr. Helen Fisher, Research Professor at Rutgers University. She says, "Casual sex might not be so casual," because both women and men can get emotionally attached after sex.[113] Clearly there are a number of possible reasons for the feeling, "I knew it was just a hookup, so why does it bother me so much that he didn't call?"

This emotional attachment may be stronger for women because of our brain chemistry. Understanding how we're "built" gives us a biological perspective as to whether casual sex works for us. But remember, nothing is simple about our brains. What follows is a very brief summary of the huge complexity of the human brain when it comes to sex.

Chemical Attraction

Dr. Helen Fisher studies the mechanisms in our brains that influence how we behave with the opposite sex, explaining our complicated desires. Her theory is that there are three mating drives:[114]

> **Lust:** a craving for sex ("I'm so horny. If Kevin doesn't make a move I'm going to jump him!")

> **Romantic love:** the feeling of desire, attraction, and infatuation in the beginning of a relationship ("Wow, Kevin is so great, I can't stand waiting until our next date!")

> **Attachment:** a feeling of security and union with a long-term partner ("I love cuddling with Kevin when we watch old movies in bed.")

Each one of these is associated with different chemicals and pathways in the brain.

Lust

The main lust hormone is testosterone.[115] Generally, testosterone causes a craving, pure and simple, for sexual gratification in both sexes.[116,117] Men have much higher testosterone levels than women,[118] and the sex centers in their brains are larger.[119] There is strong evidence to support what most women have already guessed. Men think about sex far more often than women do.[120]

Lust may propel a man towards a woman—he just wants her. But it is not what makes a woman fall in love. Brain imaging studies show that men in love have more activity in visual processing areas.[121] So they more easily fall in "love at first sight" than women. Women in love have more activity in areas related to feelings, attention, and memory.[122] Women's sexual fantasies are more focused on romance, affection, and commitment.[123] Men focus on the visual.[124]

Romantic Love

The chemicals involved are dopamine, and possibly norepinephrine and serotonin.[125] Generally, dopamine makes people feel excited, happy, "floating on air," and madly passionate. It can produce feelings of ecstasy and longing and also heightened energy. Romantic love appears to stimulate parts of the brain that are also activated when a person is using certain illicit drugs.[126] So we *can* feel "addicted to love." When reciprocated, we feel the highs of love. If not, it can feel like torture. Some say it is like an addict going through drug withdrawal. Being in love, reciprocated or not, usually involves obsessive thinking and distraction. And sometimes an uncontrollable urge to shop or excessively consume ice cream.

Attachment

The attachment chemicals are oxytocin and vasopressin.[127] They create feelings of comfort, calm, happiness, and togetherness. That's why you often hear people say things like, "Being with him feels like coming home." Sexual activity itself can trigger these attachment chemicals.[128] It can also trigger dopamine and norepinephrine, which are related to romantic love.[129] So you could also fall in love unintentionally. The very act of sex, no matter how casual we think it is, can make us feel attached because of our brain chemistry.

Remember, this is a simple version of a very complex story of human desire. We don't have all the answers. There may be other hormones involved. There is some evidence that estrogen, for example, is not only involved in female sexual desire, but it also has an effect on oxytocin (the attachment chemical).[130,131] During menopause, lower estrogen levels can impact a woman's sex life by causing vaginal dryness, fatigue, and hot flashes.[132] Cultural influences also play a role in sex and romance, as we discussed in Chapter 2. And your physiological reaction to these hormones might even depend on your genetic makeup. You may have a different set of genes that affect how oxytocin influences you than your best friend has. These genetic influences might explain our different responses to stress, attachment styles, and emotional wellbeing.[133] Studies show men and women are also different in the way vasopressin affects our bodies.[134] This might influence attachment and marital problems. Since this research is in the very early stages, don't wait for science to help you. Start to figure out your risk of getting attached by observing yourself and talking with others who know you.

One possible reason that women might have a higher risk of getting attached when we have sex is our exposure to semen. Studies show that the vagina absorbs semen, which contains many hormones.[135,136,137] Are you wondering if condoms will protect you? Nobody knows because it hasn't been studied. But don't forget that even touching and hugging can release oxytocin.[138]

Casual Sex

It's difficult to do studies about these topics. Can you imagine getting volunteers to have casual sex in order to measure their oxytocin levels? But there's been enough research to show us that, when we have sex with someone who's not relationship material, our brain can trick us into thinking he's a great guy—until it's too late.

Research on chemicals in the brain suggests a reason for the age-old saying, "Love is blind." When we are in love, the areas of the brain that are associated with social assessment of others and negative emotions are less active.[139] In other words, when we are in love, our social judgment can be impaired. No wonder we can't see the faults in our lover, even though our friends can tell he's the wrong guy. This is just one more reason for women to be cautious about sex. We could fall in love too easily even when we don't know the man very well. We are not in the best position to make a decent value judgment about whether he will be a good partner when our brains are being flooded by chemicals. Many women may be vulnerable to falling in love and getting attached when we have sex whether we like it or not, whether we want it or not.

Meanwhile, reading all these experts is likely to make anyone's eyes glaze over. I mean, if all those scientists can't even agree, how will we ever figure out what to do? So we end up in situations like Chelsea's.

Chelsea and Will had gone on several dates. Although she wasn't sure how interested she was, he made it clear he'd like to sleep with her. His obvious interest was flattering. She figured, what the heck, this time she was the one who's not that into him, so she could keep it casual. But the sex turned out to be more fun than she'd anticipated. Chelsea was bummed out when Will didn't call within a few days like he'd promised. Since it was a casual thing, she decided to call him, and she was disappointed that he didn't seem as eager to hear from her as she'd expected. But why was she so disappointed? She thought her casual approach would have protected her from getting emotionally involved.

We'll discuss protection more in the next chapter, but let's first discuss other important factors about how we're "built" that you should know before we move on.

Humanity Revisited

When the book *Fifty Shades of Grey*[140] became wildly popular, we were focused on the sex. But wasn't a big part of the draw the love story? We're also fascinated by romance and how difficult, complicated relationships work.

Relationship satisfaction depends on more than sex. For men to be happy, they have to be able to tell that their partner is happy.[141] Women have to feel that their partner is making an effort to understand their negative feelings.[142] A woman's happiness is more dependent on her partner trying to empathize with her when she feels sad or angry. For her, it's the effort to understand her unhappy emotions that counts.

David Schnarch, PhD, takes on the fundamentals of sex and intimacy in his book *Passionate Marriage: Keeping Love and Intimacy Alive in Committed Relationships.*[143] He says, "We don't realize that seeing sex as a 'drive' makes us focus on relieving sexual tensions rather than wanting our partner…if that's the only reason you think your partner wants to be with you it tends to kill sex and intimacy in marriage."[144] Regarding the teaching that men reach their sexual prime in their teens and women several years later, he says, "We've confused *genital* prime with *sexual* prime… The speed with which your body responds is only one measure of sexual prime. Your sexual peak has a great deal to do with who you are as a person. That's the point about needing to put the beauty into sex."[145] But if all you want is casual sex, what does this have to do with you?

Human beings are built for connection. Our brains need consistent bonding and nurturing. In the 1950s, Dr. Harry Harlow demonstrated how important physical touch is to the development and health of monkeys.[146] Harlow observed that infant monkeys that were raised without mothers had psychological and social deficits and clung to their fabric diapers. He then raised monkeys with both wire and wood surrogate mothers who had milk for the babies, and soft, cloth surrogate mothers who did not have any milk. The babies clung to their cloth mothers, even when they had no milk. Those that were raised with only a wire mother showed physical signs of stress, like digestive problems. Harlow concluded that babies need physical comfort from their caregivers. Many have used these studies to show the importance of physical contact and nurturing to our psychological and social development.

According to the psychiatrists who wrote *A General Theory of Love*, "We are attached to keep our brains on track."[147] They tell us the story of Holy Roman Emperor Frederick II in the 13th century, who deprived infants of human interaction to see which language they would speak. All the babies died before ever speaking. The authors (Lewis, Amini, and Lannon) say, "Evolution has sculpted mammals into their present form: they become attuned to one another's evocative signals and alter the structure of one another's nervous systems."[148]

So what does this mean to you? Think about how awful it feels when a relationship ends, the way you lose interest in everything, have trouble sleeping, or just feel lousy. Don't forget how frequent breakups disturb the rhythms of your body. We might be independent, adult women, but we haven't outgrown that basic need for connection.

Our society overlooks the emotional toll resulting from losing these attachments. Sure, breaking up is hard to do. But aren't we *supposed to* experiment when we're young to see what's out there? What are we doing to our humanity and our nervous systems with our focus on sexuality rather than love and connectedness?

What Do You Want...
and Are You Built for What You Want?

Believe it or not, some of those old-fashioned rituals make sense. Through the process of courtship, a man has to put effort into impressing a woman. She takes her time getting to know him to see if he is a genuine, trustworthy person. She lets the man pursue her. Courtship is not only more likely to give women romance, which can make us feel more desired, but it protects us from getting too involved or attached too early on. If the guy isn't interested in courting us, and he disappears, we don't risk much. If we don't require courtship, will many of us experience a series of crash-and-burn relationships? Be taken for granted? Have disappointing sex lives? Yes, if you're not being your own Brand of Sexy.

But remember, everybody's different, so think about what makes you feel desired. This will give you clarity about who you are as a person and what you are looking for in a partner.

- Do you prefer a man who romances you, or does it turn you off?

- Would you rather he pick you up at your place bearing flowers?

- Is it OK if he expects you to meet him halfway?

- Are you comfortable with him pressing for sex right away?

- Are you flattered when he calls you and sounds disappointed if you're not available?

- Does it bother you when you call him, and he says, "Uh, I'm busy. Can I call you back?"

If you're working hard to pursue him, calling him, or having uncommitted casual sex, do you feel consistently desired?

Now let's think about what you said you wanted in the last chapter—True love? Companionship? Sex without commitment?—and add in what you've just learned about how you're built. If you need to feel desired and romanced, is dating unavailable men getting what you want? If you say you just want casual sex but you're getting "hooked on your hookups," is there a disconnect between how you're built and what you think you want? See if any of these examples ring a bell:

Sandra would like to be in a committed relationship but, while she's waiting to find the right guy, she figures casual sex is better than nothing and she can handle it. These no-strings-attached relationships start out fine, but eventually Sandra starts feeling insecure ("Why isn't he calling more? Has he found someone hotter?") and clingy, wondering why she wants to see the guy more often if it's just casual.

Sandra isn't paying attention to what she needs or how casual sex affects her emotionally. She is settling for no-strings-attached sex, but she feels more attached and emotionally invested than she would like. When there is a disconnect between what we think we want and how we are built, it can cause feelings of frustration, sadness, and insecurity. Sandra could benefit from reflecting on how her decisions are not in line with her needs.

Jessica would love to be in a long-term relationship filled with romance. So she is always on the lookout for Mr. Right. She doesn't want to miss out on a great guy just because he might be shy, so if she meets someone interesting she makes sure to exchange numbers and set up a date. She's met a few men this way, but after a few dates Jessica usually starts feeling frustrated by the guy's lack of romance or effort. The relationships fizzle out, and Jessica is back on the lookout.

Jessica knows that she prefers a partner who makes romantic gestures that make her feel desired. But she consistently dates guys who do not put any effort into the relationship. By pursuing men, she is setting up the expectation that they don't have to romance her, and dating men who might not be into her. Jessica could benefit from taking a closer look at if her approach to dating is putting her on the right path toward getting what she wants.

Carly wants a relationship eventually but doesn't feel like she has time for one now. She keeps dating casually and lets men know that she's not looking for anything serious. She feels comfortable sleeping with her date if she likes him. But the sex never seems to be as good as she hoped it would be. She usually ends up feeling disappointed.

Carly thinks she is OK with casual sex. But she finds sex without intimacy or emotional connection disappointing. By letting her dates know that she's not looking for anything serious, she is telling men that they don't need to work hard to impress her or make her feel desired. Carly might experience a more fulfilling sex life if she focused more on building a relationship with a man who cares about her.

Rina has been dating Jason for a year. Most of the time things are great, but when she's upset she feels like he dismisses her feelings. It really bothers her. She doesn't want to cause problems, so she tells herself she is being unreasonable.

Rina needs to feel as though Jason is putting effort into empathizing with her emotions in order to be happy in the relationship. Instead of listening to her intuition, she talks herself out of her feelings in order to avoid conflict. If Rina were to express how she felt to Jason instead of telling herself she is being unreasonable, she might find that he is willing to work on being more understanding. If he isn't, Rina might be happier breaking things off with Jason and finding a more empathetic man. By not being honest with herself, she isn't giving herself the opportunity to find a happier relationship.

Lesley is all about having an open, honest relationship where she doesn't have to play games or pretend. So she lets guys know right away—she's looking for a long-term relationship where she can settle down with her soul mate and raise kids. And the guys run for the hills.

Lesley knows what she wants, which is a good thing. But she is so focused on her long-term relationship goals that she isn't considering who her partner is or what he wants. Understanding her own needs is important. But she must also understand the needs of her partner.

Maggie says she wants marriage and kids, but she ends up dating guys who are ambivalent about long-term commitments. She usually spends a year or so trying to figure out how to get a boyfriend to commit to her. When she finally has to break things off, she is devastated and brokenhearted, until the next commitment-phobic guy comes along.

Maggie wants one thing (commitment) but consistently does another (dates men who won't commit). Maggie could benefit from asking herself why she picks men who aren't willing to give her what she needs. Does it have something to do with her childhood? Does she have an unresolved fear of staying with one person that she hasn't acknowledged or dealt with?

For the past three years, Heather has been seeing Carl, who is unhappily married but waiting for his kids to get older before he asks for a divorce. Heather says she's fine with it; she's too focused on her career to want a commitment. But then she's surprised by how upset she gets when she "accidentally" looks in Carl's coat pocket and finds a receipt from his romantic getaway with his wife.

Like Sandra, Heather is experiencing a disconnect between what she says she wants and her emotional reaction. She says she is OK with an uncommitted relationship with Carl but finds herself feeling more attached to him than she had planned. It's important for Heather to understand how sexual intimacy affects her and to be honest with herself about her needs. Otherwise, she is setting herself up for frustration and heartache.

The Bottom Line

Let's review. How much are we hardwired? How much can we blame our parents? What is society's fault? Does it even matter? The reasons why we are the way we are aren't as important as figuring out what to do about it. We don't need these answers to figure out how to deal with the romantic situations we face. The bottom line is:

- Women are like flowers; we're all beautiful, each in our own way. We're all different, despite the similarities. For every woman who can have casual sex and be fine with it, there are plenty more who are taking a big emotional risk. But it's important to know ourselves, to know how nature and nurture shape us, so we know we're not deluding ourselves.

- Don't discard all things traditional without considering their potential value.

- Frequent breakups aren't just emotionally painful; they put our bodies on a physiological roller coaster ride.

- If you want desire and caring, whatever the reasons, you could be playing Russian roulette with your heart when you have casual sex. We're more likely to fall in love, get attached, and regret our actions than men when we have casual sex. So, if we have casual sex without getting what we want, we are losing our power.

This is our culture. A new sexual revolution can transform it but not overnight. We can change things gradually, one date at a time. Do we want to work toward a vision of equality where we all are expected to have sex "like men," or one where we can each have what we desire?

5

Protect Your Heart: Slow Can Be Sexy

*"The best protection any woman
can have is courage."*
—Elizabeth Cady Stanton

Now that you know why we need a new sexual revolution, the extent to which you're confused about the rules of dating, and how we're "built," let's move on to the next step in learning how to be your own Brand of Sexy. Think of a poker game. Why do you keep your cards close to your chest? It's not to create an air of mystery, it's to protect yourself in the game. Today, when people think about protection in dating, they think about condoms. But condoms don't protect your heart.

Are Rules Meant to Be Broken?

Maybe you think that rules are meant to be broken. It's true that the old rules were too restrictive, but they still had value. Can you imagine playing poker without any rules? There would be confusion, and someone might be taken advantage of. If your opponent said that his pair beat your royal flush, what could you do without rules? Would you challenge him? Would you feel confident enough to stand your ground? Or would he win and you feel confused? When nobody knows how the game is played, the dominant player can set the rules and have the advantage. The more trusting person is left vulnerable unless her opponent is honest. But when you first meet a guy, you don't know if he's honest. You don't know if you can trust him. He might be a nice guy, but he might not.

The game of love is like a poker game without rules, but the stakes are higher because you gamble with emotions. We're not supposed to complain about the risks involved because we're smart, strong, modern women who don't need the rules of yesteryear to protect us. Or do we?

> An independent, single woman finally has a date with the handsome, successful executive she's drooled over for weeks, and her girlfriends all give her different opinions about whether she should have sex on the first date. She decides to wear a revealing dress that makes her feel hot, and they end up going straight to his place and having wild, passionate sex. That feels great, until he changes their fancier dinner plans and takes her to an obscure, nondescript restaurant where she sees another guy she knows taking out a woman with whom he's embarrassed to be seen. So she wonders—does sex on the first date automatically lead to being taken for granted? She enjoyed the sex but is disappointed that she didn't feel special after their first date. Should she have played harder to get, or is she a modern woman who should be OK with commitment-free, casual sex?

This story probably sounds familiar to you because it's how Carrie Bradshaw and Mr. Big began their relationship on *Sex and the City*.[149] The wildly successful TV show captured the ups and downs of being a modern single woman navigating life and love. We followed the weekly antics of the colorful friends as they maneuvered their way through single life and the dating world. Although the women were different, they each had characteristics that we were able to relate to: Charlotte was the traditionalist who longed for a husband and family, Miranda was the ambitious career woman whose confidence crumbled in relationships, Samantha was the ultrastrong adventurous one who had carefree sex with abandon, and Carrie was the friend who reminded us all of ourselves (OK, maybe with more expensive shoes) and who forged ahead with her flaws, her spunk, and her questions. Just like those characters, we all have different opinions about sex. But, as pioneers facing a brand new world that has been shaped by the women's movement, the sexual revolution, and the saturation of sex in our culture, we have lost the rules that used to guide relationships. We have left ourselves unprotected emotionally.

As much as we hate and sometimes rebel against rules, we need them. Rules set the stage and often protect us. Carrie could have used some help dealing with Mr. Big. When her friends advised her, none of them talked about how Carrie could protect herself. Getting bruised emotionally was simply part of the new terrain.

Forgetting that our hearts need protection is a big mistake. Like many men today, Mr. Big didn't put any effort into his pursuit of Carrie. He started by vaguely suggesting "a drinks thing," which he then canceled at the last minute. He then brought along an upset friend to what was supposed to be a first date. But Carrie's friends never suggested that he wasn't treating her well or that having sex with him too early might be bad news. Was Mr. Big exempt from treating her well because he was successful, rich, and handsome? This was long before *Sex and the City* writer Greg Behrendt taught us that "he's just not that into you."[150]

How would you react to a situation like Carrie's? She hardly knew the guy, but she was excited about finally having a date with him. Hearing her friends' different opinions probably just increased her confusion. When some of us are confused, we practice avoidance. Others, like Carrie, jump right in without thinking about the consequences. Either way, many of us never stop to consider what's right for us before we act. And, if we do, we sometimes lie to ourselves or simply ignore our instincts because we really want the relationship to work out.

Instead of thinking about what kind of relationship she wanted—and how casual sex might not facilitate that dynamic—Carrie made an impulsive decision to sleep with Mr. Big, which colored their entire relationship. Her doubts surfaced when she made a drunken scene about the obscure restaurant and, although he offered her reassurance, their relationship was tainted by her feeling of being taken for granted. She put up with less than ideal treatment (he wouldn't introduce her to his mother, his ongoing lack of commitment) instead of being firm about her needs and expectations from the beginning, which could have protected her from getting hurt. Although Carrie and Mr. Big eventually—after countless breakups and heartache—do end up happily ever after, most relationships of that kind don't turn out quite so fairy tale-like.

Drawing a Line Requires Finding One

Where's the line between what's OK for us and what's not, what's safe and what's not, what's comfortable and what's not? We've come a long way from the '50s, when virginity until marriage was the rule. Of course our society needed change. Then, women had to live with shame if they had premarital sex. If they weren't married and got pregnant, many were shunned by family, shunted off to have their babies, and often even forced to give them up for adoption. The feeling that sex before marriage was taboo contributed to sexual problems after marriage as well. Many women couldn't just turn on their sexual desire after being conditioned into thinking for so long that sex was not OK. Others were expected to tolerate sex with their husbands in order to procreate, not to enjoy it.

In the '50s, virginity did restrict us, but it also protected us. It drew a line for us. Insisting on virginity gave us emotional distance. Without sex, we got to know a man before getting attached. Now we need all new ways to emotionally protect ourselves without returning to virginity as our only option.

One perspective on drawing the line comes from the 1995 best-seller, *The Rules: Time-Tested Secrets for Capturing the Heart of Mr. Right*.[151] The book's wisdom was supposedly from 1917 and passed down two generations. Rule #15 is "Don't Rush Into Sex," which encouraged 18-year-old virgins to wait for a committed relationship, while advising 39-year-olds that waiting for a month or two was fine. It advised all women that they can wait for marriage if they're against pre-marital sex because "if he loves you he'll respect whatever decision you make."

The Rules was a hit because it gave women permission to set limits with men and a script to follow if they weren't sure what to say. But what *The Rules* did not offer was advice on how to think through what is best for you as an individual woman or encouragement to determine what your own personal rules are. For some 39-year-olds, waiting a month before sex may be appropriate. Others may need to wait longer, and some may be comfortable with waiting less than a month. This is an extremely personal decision and warrants some consideration of what is right for you. Being your own Brand of Sexy gives you a lot more flexibility than *The Rules*. It encourages you to figure out what works for you as an individual. Based upon that, you can select the appropriate tools from the Single Woman's 12-Piece Dating Toolbox to help you further develop your own intuition and your own personal rules.

Carrie was so eager that it may have clouded her judgment about sleeping with Mr. Big. And who can blame her? When all your friends come over to celebrate a first date, it can be like a cheerleading squad ramping up the excitement. It may seem silly to suggest that peer pressure affects 30-something, grown women. But studies show that we are influenced by our peers, and that we often underestimate the effect others have on us.[152] You may think this doesn't apply to you, but low-rise jeans and frequent dieting count too!

Carrie's decision may have been wiser if her friends had approached the conversation differently. One of the biggest benefits of the sexual revolution is that sex is no longer a dirty little secret we're ashamed to discuss. We can talk about it with our friends—but now it's time to tweak that dialogue a little bit, so we can give each other better advice. We need to bring a little analysis to the table. It might seem cold and calculated, but it will bring balance to the pull of sexual chemistry and help us make better decisions.

Doctors are trained to work with our patients to balance the risks of available treatments against the potential benefits. So let's talk about risks and benefits when it comes to casual sex. As we've seen, sex makes us get attached. When we sleep with a guy we don't know well, we're much more likely to get hurt; we can't predict if he'll stick around or treat us well, so we're risking rejection, regret, embarrassment—the whole emotional roller coaster thing. (And we won't even get into the risks of sexually transmitted diseases—you've heard that many times!) Have you ever met a guy who seemed nice and then turned into a jerk or disappeared into thin air (and he wasn't a professional magician)? Face it, we all put our best foot forward at the beginning, and it's only after time that you really know what to expect from a guy.

Now for the benefits. Good sex is enjoyable (although there are no guarantees the sex will be good). And maybe it will develop into a relationship, a love affair, or at least a nice friendship. But what are the odds of that happening when you don't know the guy very well? Has that happened with you or your friends, or is a happy ending more likely when the man was more of a known quantity?

Have you heard about the "Three-Date Rule"? It's the dating rule that a woman should decide if she will consent to sex on the third date. We can't know if a man can really be trusted after only three dates. If we're held to this rule, we either have to take lots of risks, or say "no." But saying "no" can be hard. Because our culture has taught men to expect sex, we feel we should give in, and we may be afraid to lose him if we don't.

> Alison is on her third date with Kai, who has made it clear he wants to sleep with her. Kai is an outgoing, personable guy who loves to strike up conversations with other people, and Alison can't tell if he's flirting with other women or if she's misinterpreting his friendliness. She doesn't feel comfortable having sex in a nonexclusive relationship but isn't sure she wants to be exclusive with a guy who might be a major flirt or player. Yet she's afraid to say "no" and lose her chance with him, in case he turns out to be a nice guy.

Weighing risks and benefits just doesn't seem sexy. Besides, many of us act first and think later—the "uh-oh" phenomenon.

Consider these questions:

1. How will you feel if you have sex and he disappears off the face of the Earth?

2. What if he treats you very differently (no more dates, just booty calls)?

3. What if he's really not that into you?

4. How much will you regret passing on sex
   if you never hear from him again?

OK, some of you may feel like these aren't serious consequences, and it's all no big deal. Maybe the closer you get to
wanting a serious relationship, the more you naturally guard
your heart because you've seen all the time and emotional
energy you can spend on a guy who's not into you. But how
many times do you get hurt or frustrated along the way until
you start naturally guarding your heart? As we've become
more immune to the sexualization of our culture, we've also
become more sensitized to the "no biggie" aspect of having
casual sex and of the repercussions.

We think that's "just the way it is" with less risky situations
as well. We don't have to get to the point of sexual involve-
ment to consider the idea of protecting ourselves or thinking
about how we feel and what we want. It's hard to figure out
where the line is in all kinds of dating situations. So let's take
a broader look at the reality of dating.

Reality or Delusion?

Nothing epitomizes the problems of modern dating quite
like reality TV shows like *The Bachelor*. Here, a large group of
beautiful women compete for the man, which is a complete
role reversal from traditional dating expectations. He doesn't
have to lift a finger to woo them, or prove he's interesting,
charming, or even a nice guy. The women are the ones who
have to prove themselves. Some grow emotionally involved
so, when they're booted from the show, they feel like they've
been jilted from a serious relationship (as if they were on an
actual, extended date instead of a reality show).

Interestingly, the show *The Bachelorette* has a better success
rate of couples staying together.[153] Is it possible that something works better for relationships when we are the ones

being courted? Sadly, *The Bachelor* actually mirrors our society today. Many women feel it is up to them to ask men out, to pay for dates, to sleep with guys without commitment, and to live with them without marriage, without expecting anything in return. Some actually make the case that these changes indicate that we're the ones with the power. But wait—aren't we just making it easier for some not-so-nice men to take us for granted? No wonder we can't tell if they're not that into us before they break our hearts. We're no longer making it clear to men that we have expectations too.

But didn't the women's movement mean we were equal to men, so shouldn't we take the initiative—and take risks—in love? Look at that question again. Why is there a "should" in it? Why are we making decisions based on what we feel we "should" do? Based on political correctness rather than our unique feelings? Expecting women to ignore their emotions is denying our individuality—which is actually what the women's movement was all about, not simply saying men and women were the same. As Gloria Steinem said, "A feminist is anyone who recognizes the equality and full humanity of women and men."[154]

Feminism isn't the problem. It's how we translate it. We just threw away one set of rules (women should stay home and be wives and mothers, subservient to their husbands) and accepted another set of rules (women should act just like men). But both deny our own unique, emotional needs.

We're long overdue for a dialogue on this subject. Are women more equal when we give up our power, competing for a man's attention without having any expectations? Remember, before the women's movement, women blindly accepted their culturally assigned roles. Some didn't recognize when societal norms left them unhappy or unfulfilled, while others felt powerless to change their situation. Are we that different today? Don't we accept our culture's sexual mores even when they leave us unfulfilled? We feel we have no choice because that's "just the way it is." We don't stop to ask what is best for us as individuals—we're too busy trying to fit in.

In the past, we might have felt frustrated when we were attracted to a man and couldn't call him because "women can't make the first move." Now society gives us that freedom but, for some women, the customs of the past may still be useful. Waiting for the man to call does give you some information about how interested he is in you—if he calls, at least he's interested enough to risk possible rejection. And many men get the wrong idea when a woman calls them first. Have you noticed some men only need a smile from a woman to decide she's "hot for him"? If you actually ask him out, some guys may figure you've already signaled your interest in sex and he can skip the usual preliminaries. But is that what you intended? The goal here is not to force a man to fake preliminaries but to make it easier for you to tell whether he's really interested. If he has a few minor hoops to jump through, he's at least proving he's willing to put himself out there a little.

There are still plenty of men who want committed relationships with women. The trick is how to protect yourself from getting burned as much as possible before you discover what kind of man he really is. It isn't always easy to tell if a guy truly wants a relationship. Even if he says he does, some men just can't pull it off. The better your instincts, intuition, and ability to protect yourself, the easier and more fun dating can be.

Men are getting used to women taking the initiative; many of them assume a woman who calls is easily within reach, so they don't have to work to get her. And sure, not all men take casual sex for granted. He could be a really nice guy but, until you get to know him, how can you tell for sure? Without societal rules and guidelines, we have to be skilled at figuring out where and how to draw the line to protect ourselves.

Some of us are blessed with good instincts and good insights into what works for us, and others of us are not. If you don't know for sure if he is a good man or what is going to work for you, it's probably best to play it safe. We like to blame the media for society's problems. We forget they're reflecting our lives and what we want to know about in the world. If everyone decided *Sex and the City* was too risqué for TV, or *The Bachelor* was unfair to women, those shows would be canceled. But we're dying to see what happens next or to live vicariously. Meanwhile we're conflicted— we say we want to be desired, but we pursue emotionally unavailable, commitment-phobic men. What do we want?

Bringing Sir Galahad Back from the Dead?

Some say chivalry is dead. Some men simply aren't raised to open doors for ladies, pull out their chairs before they sit, or help them with their luggage. And some are afraid to try it because they've been scolded for doing so. Women have been offended by their displays of gallantry, so many stop trying. Wouldn't you do the same if, when you are trying to help someone, it lands you a dirty look or a complaint? We're not sure what equality means. Do we have to be more like men? Are we helpless if we let him help us? Or are we making things harder than they need to be? If you make half the salary of your date, should you offer to split the bill in order to feel equal? What if you make twice what he makes? Should a petite woman feel conflicted if she lets a man help her because she can't get her suitcase into the airplane's overhead compartment? If a man opens your door, do you have to wonder if there's a hidden meaning? No, of course not—there's nothing wrong with getting help with your bag, letting your date display interest in you, or allowing a polite gesture of kindness. (Don't you enjoy helping other people sometimes?)

Some gallant men might just be nice guys. We can enjoy these things and still feel equal, modern, and self-sufficient. In fact, there are times when a little chivalry would make a big difference:

> Shoshanna Shapiro, a character on HBO's series, *Girls*, reveals the "biggest baggage" she has—her virginity.[155] Her shame pushes her to lose her v-card as soon as possible, throwing caution to the wind. In the bedroom, while she wears only matching lingerie, David rejects her because she's a virgin, saying rather unsympathetically, "I'm totally fine having sex with you once you've already had sex, but virgins just aren't my thing."[156] And when she protests, he says, "It's just like virgins get attached. Or they bleed."[157] The show doesn't address how she feels about this encounter, but it seems likely it would have compounded her shame.

If chivalry is dead, has romance been mortally wounded? Isn't there something nice about struggling with a very large suitcase and having a big, strong man come to your rescue? Do we really want to *miss out* on those experiences? Not only are we cutting ourselves off from something that might make a man appealing to us, and might add a touch of romance to our lives, we're training men to be less nice to us. How can this be helpful? If some amount of chivalry sparks romantic feelings in us, then why would we want to lose it? If feeling desired is so critically important to our sexuality, why are we pushing it away? There are times when being politically correct is emotionally incorrect.

The muddled dynamics of love and romance make it hard to figure out what cards you have, much less how to play them. The problem is that, if you do want a guy's help nowadays, you may have to ask for it. We're conflicted about wanting his help because we're supposed to be independent, self-sufficient women, believing, as Gloria Steinem said, "a woman without a man is like a fish without a bicycle."[158] Are we carrying it too far? Does anybody want to bring chivalry back from the dead?

We're so pressured to have sex today that some women are rejecting men *before* the first date because "I wouldn't want to sleep with him." Do we have to decide when we first *see* him? Must we rob ourselves of the possibility of experiencing a little courtship from a nice guy because we already feel obligated to decide about sex? Not to mention depriving the nice guys of a chance to woo us, and letting the hot, rich ones have so many options that they can get away with treating women poorly. What if we could simply let the man try to convince us of his worthiness, interest, and good character? If we can have no-strings-attached sex as modern women, why can't we have no-strings-attached courtship?

Of course most of us aren't looking for paternalistic protection anymore, but we still want men to be accountable for their actions. Are we giving mixed messages? We act like accountability is no big deal when we date the bad boys and when we have sex without the commitment we want. Maybe what's really going on is that we're no longer clear about what are reasonable behaviors to expect from men and whether we deserve to expect what we want. We're confused pioneers, trying to figure out how to maneuver all the changes in our culture. Many of us have stopped drawing the line for men. We call them, ask them out, have sex without commitment, "hook up," and think it's normal if we have to wait for the commitment we want, even if we're unhappy with the situation. How are men supposed to figure out what we want if we aren't clear? If we aren't sure where the line is, won't some men step over it every time?

Jodi and Theo are pals who go out for a few beers one Friday night and end up at Theo's place. The next morning, she offers to make him some breakfast, but he makes up transparent excuses to get her to leave ("I have an early conference call") and, when she gets upset, he can't figure out why since it was just a casual hookup.

One of the biggest casualties of the sexual revolution has been romance. Since we don't know if there are any differences between us, men don't know how much courtship is required and women aren't sure it's OK to want romance. We saw in Chapter 1 how successful romance novels are, and don't overlook the tremendous popularity of Jane Austen books and movies.[159] Isn't it possible we love them so much because we feel deprived of romance and courtship? Remember, for women, sex is still not separate from intimacy. Why are we tolerating behaviors that would have never been acceptable in the past?

Expect Respect

Most men know when they're treating women badly. OK, so maybe the young ones have been raised in such an environment of politically correct equality that they think gallantry might offend a woman. And so many women have trained men to stop treating them well that men are confused. So anybody who wants to bring chivalry back must consider some ways to encourage men to keep up the things we like. We must expect respect. This is one of the ways we can change the world, one date at a time. If he's into you, you'll see results. If he's not that into you, he probably won't bother. It's true you'll have one less guy to date, but it will also be one less aggravating situation in your life.

Expecting respect may require retraining and restraining ourselves. We're so used to doing what we think we "should" do to be modern, independent, equal women that we don't consider how we feel about the relationship or whether we feel like we're treated in a special way by the man. And we believe that, as strong women, if we know what we want, then we should "go for it!" But "going for it" can create problems if the guy isn't treating you well. Sometimes you need to take a step back, slow down, and let the guy prove to you that he's worth going for. Otherwise, we can end up in relationships with men who don't treat us with respect. And when that happens, it's like we're telling ourselves, "I don't deserve anything better." Sure, we may never get *everything* we want in a relationship, but where is the room for negotiation if we start with the idea that what we want is *way* too much to expect? The bar is already pretty low—when we start compromising, how much lower can it go? No wonder we aren't pleased with the results. How will we ever get what we want if we tell ourselves we don't deserve it?

Obviously, this retraining involves learning how to say "no." You probably already know how, but sometimes it's hard to do it, especially if you like the guy and are afraid you'll lose him. We'll talk more about this in the next chapter but, for now, let's look at the lives of two women with very different approaches so you can see for yourself which is more appealing to you.

Janine would love a long-term relationship, so she dates lots of guys, figuring it improves her odds. She wants to be seen as easy to get along with, and she figures she can't expect much without a commitment, so she doesn't complain when her dates' behavior bothers her—calling on Thursday for a Friday night, or showing up late when they have a date. She starts seeing Dennis exclusively, and she likes having a boyfriend, but she's noticed that he seems to be taking her for granted; he rarely compliments her, and he assumes that, since they're a couple, they can have "hangout dates" rather than nice nights out. Plus, he never offers to come to her place, which leaves her always having to make the drive to his apartment.

After getting fed up with having her heart broken by commitment-phobic, inconsiderate, immature men, Tara read a self-help book and got some good ideas, which she added to her own gut instincts. Her guidelines eliminate men who are going to be trouble or who don't seem really interested. This leaves her with fewer dates, but they are all higher-quality men who treat her well. At first she doesn't know what to do with the free time she used to spend on mediocre dates. But then she starts enjoying some of her old hobbies again, like salsa dancing. And, at a recent class, she met the nicest guy. She resisted the temptation to make the first move and, sure enough, he called her.

Being your own Brand of Sexy means expecting respect. When you know what you want and what works for you, then you can hold out for the kind of treatment you want and deserve. When you can learn to draw a line, men get clear signals about what you want. So, either they will try to please you, or they'll disappear—which makes it very easy for you to tell who's into you and who's not. And if you don't feel that confident yet, don't worry—keep reading. You won't transform every inconsiderate frog into a chivalrous prince. But, by training yourself to say "no" to behavior you don't find acceptable, at least you'll stop letting those frogs waste your time.

Risky Business

Last but definitely not least, let's discuss some of the major impediments to successfully implementing this step. The scientists *all* agree on this one point: Alcohol and drugs definitely loosen your inhibitions and impair your judgment, and they can interact with other medications you may be taking to make that single drink much more potent. Read the information about any medication you take, no matter how harmless it seems. If it hasn't happened to you, it's probably happened to someone you know. You didn't mean to sleep with him, but you got carried away, or you said something you regret. Knowing your tolerance with intoxicating substances is very important. When in doubt, be more protective of yourself. It's amazing how much more appealing a jerky guy can seem after a few tequila shooters, but you want to like him when you're sober too!

Protecting Ourselves

Forgetting to protect our hearts is a big mistake. Once upon a time, our parents looked out for us. Then dating and courtship rules protected us, but now we need to do it for ourselves. Carrie may have thought her great dress and sassy attitude were all she needed on her date with Mr. Big. But as she soon learned, she should have protected herself with more than a condom. She may have gotten her fairy-tale ending, but she endured years of misery putting up with Big's unacceptable behavior. The fairy-tale ending doesn't have to come with that price.

Although independent, single female characters existed on TV a few decades ago, their sexual activity was taboo. ("That Girl" and "Mary Tyler Moore" had plenty of dates, but we never saw more than a chaste good-night kiss.) Thanks to the women's movement and the sexual revolution, we've broken free of stereotypes and restrictions. Characters like Carrie, Charlotte, Miranda, and Samantha can now openly discuss sex. Although we imagined this new freedom would solve all our problems, we didn't realize we'd be creating new ones by ignoring the protections we lost. We end up gambling with our emotions in a risky game of love without any rules. So now we need a *new* sexual revolution to find new ways to protect ourselves.

We'll be exploring in greater detail how we can protect ourselves early in the relationship in the next few chapters. This book is designed to be like a buffet: Whether you want tips on how to expect respect or ideas about how to be your own Brand of Sexy, the choice is yours. Being your own Brand of Sexy will look a little different for each of us because we're all unique. Change can be very hard, but it becomes much easier when you take it in small steps. To decide what's best for you, consider your comfort level, what you want to change in your life, and what you want to change in the world—one date at a time.

6

Emotional Hygiene: Your Voice Matters

*"Knowing yourself
is the beginning of wisdom."*
—Aristotle

To be your own Brand of Sexy, you might have to start with some soul-searching. Self-help books can only do so much because they're one-size-fits-all. Being your own Brand of Sexy is all about what's best for you as an individual. It's really hard to be objective about ourselves—which is why we have so much trouble seeing what's getting in our way. But remember—you're the gardener of your soul. Some flowers thrive with lots of sun, while some need water and shade. Similarly, each of us has unique emotional needs, and your needs might be very different from those of your friends. It's important to take the time to learn and pay attention to what works for you.

If you neglect your emotional needs, how will you ever fully blossom as a woman? We get our hair cut, styled, colored, permed, and straightened; our nails polished; and our skin peeled and plumped. And we're looking good, all right. But that's only the shell of who we are. Sure, society says that shell better be looking good, but is skin-deep beauty more important than inner beauty? Isn't there more to you than an attractive face and body? If we spent as much time on our inner beauty, we'd all be masters of enlightenment. And, if we don't listen to our inner wisdom, we're more likely to be swayed by peers, media, science books, self-help books, and—last but not least—men.

By the way, don't be surprised if you find yourself getting distracted or impatient with this chapter. When something pushes our buttons (maybe by striking us as too close for comfort), our gut reaction can be to back away because dealing with emotions can be difficult and painful. But it's also a signal that what you're reading has hit a nerve, so give yourself a minute to look at what you're feeling. (It's like when you finally start flossing your teeth—the first time might hurt, but you know it's good for you and it gets easier every time!)

How Do You Feel? Getting in Touch With Your Emotions

How do you feel on the inside? Beneath your good-looking exterior, what do you want? Feelings and thoughts help guide us. They are the keys to knowing who we are and what's important to us. If a guy says something that makes you angry, it's probably a signal that he's crossed a line with you. But feelings and thoughts can also sabotage us. If you're so furious with him that you tell him off, he may have trouble hearing you because he sees you as irrational.

Our emotions can sometimes be difficult to identify. Defenses are psychological strategies that we all use, consciously and unconsciously, to protect ourselves from distressing feelings. Conscious defenses are those that you are aware of and deliberately employ ("I don't have time to think about the breakup today. I'll think about it tomorrow"), while unconscious defenses are automatic coping strategies that you may not even be aware of. Often, these develop in child-hood to handle difficult situations and persist into adulthood. Denial is one type of unconscious defense that most of us are familiar with.

Defenses help us cope with everyday life. Imagine going to work after a breakup without any defenses. How productive would you be if you felt sad every minute and all you could think about was, "What will life be like without him?" You'd never get anything done. But they can also make it difficult for you to be aware of how you feel. If a guy stops calling you, doesn't return your calls or texts, and you hear that he's dating other people, but you are still convinced that he is your Mr. Right, your unconscious is employing denial to protect you from the blow of rejection. In doing so, it may be difficult for you to recognize your true emotions—perhaps deep down you are scared of rejection and hurt, and you're disappointed that Mr. Right turned out to be Mr. Wrong.

On top of the confusion caused by defenses, some of our parents weren't good at talking about feelings, so they couldn't teach us how to identify them. A fear of getting in touch with emotions can make it even harder. Don't worry—you can still learn how.

There are clues about how we're feeling from our thoughts: "What if he never calls again? What if he sleeps with some-one else? I can't date a man who has kids because it never works out with those guys." Doesn't this sound like someone who's scared of losing a guy? Our fears may be unfounded or we might be overreacting, but they still have value. They teach us something about ourselves. Sometimes we aren't even aware of the things we tell ourselves out of fear that interfere with getting what we want.

Maylin wants to be in a long-term relationship eventu-ally. Meanwhile, she's dating Seth, who's attractive, fun, and somewhat unpredictable. After a few dates, he tells her he's "not very good at relationships." Sometimes he makes plans with her for Saturday night, but sometimes she doesn't hear from him for over a week. She has a gut sense that he isn't great at commitment, but she figures, "Oh, well, at least he's being honest," and continues seeing him. At the same time, she doesn't understand why she feels so frustrated.

Emotional hygiene is like brushing your teeth—it's a way to prevent emotional problems. It takes time and energy to figure out how we're feeling, what we're thinking, and whether we're sabotaging ourselves or not. Are we letting culture or friends steer us off course? We can't always tell how we feel by our actions. If we're scared, we might seem super cautious about getting involved, or we might rush into a relationship.

Here are some of the more obvious feelings you may have experienced in the dating process. If it's hard for you to identify your feelings, the following thoughts might resonate with you and help you connect with a feeling. Listen to what you say to yourself.

Discouragement: "Another one bites the dust. When will I ever meet anybody? It's a jungle out there!"

Infatuation: "Oh, my god, he's so gorgeous! He's smart, funny, and successful—in fact, he's the nicest guy I've ever met. I bet he'd be a fantastic father too."

Sadness, disappointment: "I really liked him. I thought we really clicked. I'll just watch a rerun of (sad movie)."

Excitement: "He actually DID call! He's reliable AND he's interested. Now I'll have a presentable date for my cousin's wedding!"

Hopelessness: "I'll never find a boyfriend. I'll be alone forever. When I die, I'll be a crabby old lady, living alone in an apartment with 25 cats."

Confidence: "I have a lot to offer in a relationship. I'm good company. I feel really good about myself, inside and out. If he doesn't call, he wasn't the right one for me."

Anger at self: "What's wrong with me? Guys just don't find me attractive. They don't want me because I'm too fat/thin/old/young/quiet/loud/neurotic/boring (fill in the appropriate word)."

Anger at men: "What a jerk! All men are creeps. I'm never dating again."

When we begin to see glimpses of our feelings, we still may not use them to guide our behavior. Often we have concerns about a guy, and then talk ourselves out of those concerns by making excuses for him. Do any of these sound familiar to you?

- "Sure, he's a little immature, but he's so smart."

- "He doesn't have a lot of time for me, but hey, he works for a startup."

- "He never apologizes when he hurts my feelings, but he's so hot, and he's a great dancer."

- "He's self-centered and thinks he's always right, but that's how his parents raised him. I'm sure he'll learn to be more considerate eventually."

- "Well, he does sleep with other women, but we're both too modern to be bound by old-fashioned standards of monogamy."

- "Maybe he's not that into me, but that'll change once he gets to know me better."

- "He didn't call like he promised, but why should I be hurt? He's a hookup, not my boyfriend."

- "He can't commit, but he says his ex-girlfriend did a number on him, and he's really working on it."

You know what happens when you start excusing his behavior. You ignore how you feel, letting him take you for granted and avoiding the fact that he's probably going to break your heart. This is how so many of us end up with guys who just aren't that into us. But what's even worse is that what you are really saying is, "My feelings don't count" or "I don't deserve any better."

Mind Games

Ever heard of a mindset? It's a collection of thoughts and feelings that determine your approach to challenging situations. Dating is like finding a job. But, assuming you want a relationship, dating is even more likely to push our buttons. You don't necessarily have to feel attractive or lovable to find a job. Finding a relationship taps into all our insecurities. The process requires a lot of time and energy, and the ups and downs can be very emotional. It helps to have an effective way to manage your thoughts and feelings.

Dr. Carol Dweck presents a helpful perspective in her book, *Mindset: The New Psychology of Success*, in which she explains the two different mindsets people may have.[160] Those with a "fixed mindset" believe their abilities are set in stone, so they view every dating encounter as a test of their worth and every mistake as a failure. People with a "growth mindset" believe their abilities can improve, so they think of their interactions with possible dates (and possible mistakes) as learning opportunities. Dweck encourages her readers to cultivate a growth mindset.

Here's how these different mindsets can affect how we deal with the challenges of dating:

Amanda has been going out with Darius for about two months, when he tells her he doesn't think they're right for each other. She decides it's because she's not pretty enough—after all, she knows she has average features and she isn't in the best shape. She should be working out more. Why would any guy be attracted to her in the first place, and what's the point of even dating when no guy is really going to want her?

Chen has been going out with Alex for about two months, when he tells her he doesn't think they're right for each other. At first she's hurt and starts to get down on herself, but then she talks it over with some friends. She realizes that he was a little shy, and she may have come on a bit too strong at the beginning, letting him know how much she liked him and joking on their second date about what they should name the kids. She decides to play it a bit cooler next time. She's just glad she figured that out before she got too emotionally involved.

What does your fixed mindset look like?

- "I have to find a man! My clock is ticking."
- "I can't find a man."
- "All men are creeps and losers."
- "I must have done something wrong."
- "Guys don't find me attractive;
  I need to lose weight before I can date."

Can you see why these mindsets might interfere with a successful outcome? If you feel desperate, or you're furious with men, they will notice. Men steer clear of us when we radiate negativity and low self-esteem, which then reinforces the negative, fixed mindset ("See, I was right, I'm not attractive and there are no decent guys out there anyhow").

Although a ticking clock is a biological reality, you don't have to be desperate to find a man. Why not decide whether you want to and if you are emotionally and financially prepared to have a child instead? Would you feel comfortable doing this on your own? Consider all your options, not simply a man solving the problem.

Dating can be difficult. Dry spells, rejection, and disappointment are the name of the game. Sometimes the process becomes so discouraging that we forget the good parts about being single. Believe it or not, remembering the upside can be helpful. In a relationship, you commit a lot more time and energy to someone else, so you have much less time for yourself. The silver lining of being single is that it's an opportunity to grow, discover yourself, get new hobbies, make new friends, travel—do the things you've always wanted to do. It can be hard to change your perspective but, when you're exploring the world, you're more likely to meet interesting men—and you're in a better state of mind to meet one.

Maybe Americans do have a battle-of-the-sexes mentality but, when a guy dumps you, you may feel like you deserve to declare war! Anger is a normal reaction to loss, and we're much more likely to be angry when we're unceremoniously dumped. The problem arises when we have trouble letting go of our anger. We certainly don't want anger to seep into our interactions with men who have done no wrong. Studies say forgiveness helps us move on and is much healthier, even if it's difficult.[161] What can we tell ourselves?

- "I can't let this breakup consume me."

- "I need to move on. That poor guy has major issues, and maybe he did me a favor by breaking it off."

- "He isn't the right partner for me."

So what's the most useful mindset? One that acknowledges the challenges involved in dating but in an optimistic way ("I know what I want, and I'm on the road toward getting it"). And, when things don't work out, a growth mindset acknowledges the disappointment while looking for opportunities to grow ("That breakup really hurt, but what can I learn from this mess?"). Nora Ephron said it well: "Above all, be the heroine of your life, not the victim."[162] Remember, with a growth mindset, dating can be fun, or at least a learning experience—if you replace "Men are creeps and losers" with "What can I learn from this situation?"

When feelings cloud our judgment, bringing a little thought to the table can help us have a more accurate perspective of the situation. That's why talking to friends, family, and therapists can help if we're going to extremes, either too emotional or overly analytical. They give us the big picture while we're thinking we got rejected because we're too fat. When we can calm down and tune out the negative chatter, it becomes much easier to tune in to the nuances of how we feel and what we think.

If you expect true love on every date, you will be disappointed. If you approach the date realistically and with a growth mindset, you may actually have fun and learn something as well. Why not get to know the guy and look past your first impression? Maybe he can teach you something about computers if he seems like a tech guy or about finance if he seems cheap. If he's nervous, maybe he finds you hot, which you can take as a compliment. If you don't like his looks, maybe your friend will. If he's a jerk, you can practice being playful when you stand up for yourself, a skill that always comes in handy with men who test us to see how much they can get away with. You will always have a positive experience if your attitude is: "I am going to have fun, no matter where I go or who my date is. Either I will learn something, or else

I will be able to entertain my friends with my stories." Dating can be a wonderful experience. It is always more enjoyable if you like yourself and can find something appealing about your date. When you are overly critical of yourself or your date, it spells misery.

Obsessionland

Ladies, step right up and get your tickets to Obsessionland, a magical place where you get to think about a guy 24/7. Try to read his mind! Drive yourself crazy by processing everything he says and does! Worry about his motives! Spend sleepless hours deciding whether or not to call, text, or email him! And drive yourself crazy wondering:

- "I wish I knew whether he had a good time with me last night."

- "I wonder when he's going to call me."

- "Should I call just to see if he's OK, or will that feel like stalking?"

- "Has he gotten super busy at work? And does that mean he's a workaholic?"

- "I bet he's started seeing someone else who's thinner/prettier/more fun than I am!"

- "What if he's too insecure and, if I don't call, he'll freak out and disappear?"

- "He never wants to see me again, and I'll be alone for the rest of my life."

Those of us who have visited Obsessionland learned the hard way that it's not a healthy place to go (but oh, it's hard to resist: endlessly analyzing your love interest is as tempting as chocolate!). Obsession is an emotional pendulum that swings between cloud nine when he calls and heartache when he doesn't. It puts your happiness in the hands of a man, and it's a frustrating and painful place to be. Such a narrow focus limits other areas of your life, consumes your time and energy, and affects your relationships with friends and family. And, when you obsess over a man, it becomes difficult to see his flaws, making you vulnerable to an unhealthy romantic relationship. Simply put: Obsessing about a man is dangerous to your health!

Obsessing isn't helpful when dating and can in fact make things worse: If he finally does call you, you're more likely to sound tense or overly eager. It's critical to figure out how to calm yourself down and reassure yourself. Many women find it helpful to talk to friends, mothers, or therapists. Maybe it helps you relax to take a hot bath or to be in nature. Keeping a journal helps many of us get a better perspective and work through the emotional baggage. Obsession obscures our ability to figure out if the guy is even *worth* worrying about. (And, if you still have trouble leaving Obsessionland, we'll discuss it further in Chapter 9.)

However, sometimes a touch of obsession is informative. Maybe you're scared of getting hurt because your last breakup was so awful. Sometimes it's a signal that there is something this man is doing that is really bothering you. It might be a message to you that you need to stand up for yourself, but you're having a hard time realizing it or doing it.

> Brianna has gone out a few times with Tad. They seemed to get along great, but then he doesn't call her for over a week. She can't stop thinking about him—did he get tired of her? Is he seeing someone else? Should she check to see if he's had an accident? She leaves him a message and, when he doesn't call back right away, she figures it's hopeless and drowns her sorrows in Mocha Java Chip ice cream, remembering the misery of her last breakup. The next day

he calls and explains that he had a last-minute business trip but is back and would love to see her. Now Brianna has two days to lose the Häagen-Dazs weight, analyze the tone of his voice over the phone, plan the perfect outfit for their date, and drive herself crazy figuring out how to act when she sees him.

Kayla has gone out a few times with Adam, who doesn't call her for over a week. At first Kayla is frantic wondering what happened but, after talking to her girlfriends, she realizes it really bothers her that he never asks her out for Saturday night. Rather than drive herself nuts, she signs up for the salsa dance class she'd been meaning to start. A week later Adam does call, explaining he'd gotten really busy at work, and he asks her out for Friday. Although it bugs her to accept another Friday night date, she's looking forward to seeing him again.

Here are some thoughts that might provide a little reassurance to you when you're in this strange land:

- "I deserve a guy who will pursue me."
- "I can figure out why he cancelled later— right now I am going to make some other plans."
- "This is good practice."
- "I'm so sad, but maybe he did me a favor."
- "I don't want a guy who's not into me."
- "Maybe he just got really busy and I'll hear from him eventually."
- "Everyone has something to teach me."
- "I don't have to freak out if he doesn't call every day."

More Than a Feeling: Intuition

One of your most valuable assets is your intuition. It's like having a crystal ball giving you a peek into the future. It can help you size up a man's character, let you know when you're in danger, and help you relax when you're safe. Being aware of your feelings in reaction to him brings a dose of reality to your romantic illusions and assumptions. How do you feel if he's critical of you or others? If he downs one drink and orders a second before you've ordered dinner, are you concerned? If you say to yourself, "But he's so cute, that doesn't really matter," aren't you ignoring a potential problem?

Intuition is our "sixth sense," telling us something is off even if we're not quite sure why. Have you ever had a gut feeling that you ignored, and then ended up regretting it? ("I knew I shouldn't have done that, but I didn't listen to myself!") While sometimes it works to go with your gut, it can also lead you astray. Feelings aren't always clear-cut. Sometimes feelings steer you wrong. One way this happens is unconsciously (e.g., if you hate all men because your father hurt you deeply as a child, this will muddle your instincts and possibly make you more frightened about getting hurt by men or more mistrustful of them without good reason). We'll discuss more how to tell whether your gut instincts are working for you or against you as this chapter progresses and in future chapters.

But when it works well, intuition is like an internal global positioning system (GPS), a navigational tool that helps guide us in the direction we want to go. We may make an occasional wrong turn, but a good GPS gently says, "Recalculating!" It assesses the situation and figures out the next steps. All we need to do is tune into that "sixth sense." Here are a couple of examples so you can see what messages your intuition sends you:

Scenario 1: Imagine yourself dating a guy who always says the right thing, but something feels a bit off. One night he's driving you home when another car cuts him off and he goes ballistic. Do you think, "So he's got a hot temper, but I'd be crazy to dump a guy who's really into me?" Or do you get a gut sense that he might be been presenting you a false front and wonder what else he's hiding?

Scenario 2: The guy you're dating is generous with you, bringing you flowers, taking you to nice restaurants, and insisting on paying, but you notice he's rude to the waiters and leaves skimpy tips. Do you figure he's just demanding, and secretly slip a bit extra to the waiter, or do you think, "Hmm, he may be wealthy, but I don't like how he treats other people, and that's a big red flag"?

What about a first date who wants to pick you up at your house? You don't know the guy very well, so you're not comfortable with that, but you're afraid to hurt his feelings or push him away. Do you think, "Oh, come on, he's probably fine, and I'm just being too uptight"? Or do you tell him you'd rather meet him someplace until you get to know him better?

How do you proceed with caution? This brings us to the subject of sexual feelings. Ever heard of delayed gratification? It's not popular these days to wait to have sex, but it can be helpful. It protects you from guys who aren't that into you and guys who can't commit, and it saves you from those emotional roller coaster rides. Have you heard about or directly experienced the "uh-oh" phenomenon, in which you get carried away and make a poor choice about sex? Sometime later, you wonder why you did it and might regret the experience. Frequently, alcohol or drugs are part of the problem, causing some impairment of judgment. That's why protecting yourself emotionally also involves limiting or stopping your use of alcohol and/or drugs. As we saw in Chapter 4, sex clouds our judgment about men. It's a sure way to sabotage your intuition.

Can You Trust Your Instincts?

Let's look at your instincts for a minute. There's a big difference between animal instincts, the sexual feelings we might have for a guy, and our protective instincts—that little warning bell that goes off in your head that says, "Uh, oh, he just told me he cheated on his last girlfriend but would never do it again. Should I be worried he'll do the same with me?" Now it's possible that your animal instincts could be in conflict with your protective instincts ("He's so hot. Maybe it's not important if he cheated. I just want a fling"). Ignoring your protective instincts can get you into trouble. As many of us have learned the hard way, that hookup could lead to months or years of being in love with a guy who cheats.

In the old days, women were supposed to squelch their animal urges, follow the rules, and wait for marriage. Today our issues are turned upside down. We're encouraged to have sexual feelings, and our protective instincts aren't encouraged. Undoubtedly, those sexual feelings can lead to a sexual experience that might not be a good emotional choice. But if you have a pattern of saying, "My hormones made me do it," it may not be your sex drive that's the problem. Maybe you're afraid of commitment, or perhaps you're working through some childhood issues. After all, your coupled friends have sex too—they just seem to have sex with guys who can and do commit. You may be choosing men who aren't emotionally available.

If you're sexually attracted to nice guys and turned off by players, you're lucky—your instincts are more likely to lead you to what you want. But if you are more turned on by the "bad boys," you probably need to develop the protective side of your instincts. Often this involves delaying sex, which can be tough. We're an instant-gratification society, and we want what we want right away. Many of us want a boyfriend, and when we meet a new man our animal instincts encourage us to have sex even though we don't know yet if he can be trusted or if he will treat us well. Delayed gratification is one of the best tools in our arsenal to protect ourselves and to hone our protective instincts.

> Luciana and George worked in the same building, and every time she ran into him her knees got weak (tall, dark, and really cute!). After weeks of elevator-flirting, they went on a few dates and hit it off. For the third date, he invited her to his place, which made her uncomfortable, since she'd heard he was a bit of a "player." But she was so attracted to him, and she figured, "We'll probably do it eventually anyhow," so they ended up having sex. She thought they'd had a great time and he said he'd call her again, but he never did.

> Bethany and Matt had gone out a few times and things had gone pretty well; this time, he invited her over for a quiet dinner at his place. Bethany liked him and even felt attracted to him, but she just didn't know him well enough to have sex yet. So she told him she'd love to see him again, but she wasn't quite ready to go to his apartment. Matt made it clear that he was disappointed, but he liked her enough to respect her wishes.

Looking for Patterns

One of the most helpful emotional hygiene exercises is to consider whether you are repeating certain situations in your life. Seeing a pattern in the type of men you date or how you behave with them can help you figure out the problems you need to address to greatly improve your dating life. Believe it or not, often people find themselves in similar predicaments in their love lives as they do at work. For example, many women who take care of others' feelings at the expense of their own feel taken for granted at work, with their families, and with the men they date.

Do any of these patterns ring a bell?

- Putting his feelings ahead of yours ("I don't like how he's treating me lately, but I need to give him some space, he's really stressed out at work.")

- Attraction to unavailable men ("The only guys who aren't commitment-phobic are really boring.")

- Going for superficial attributes rather than any real connection ("Who cares if our conversations aren't great, he's really hot and he's successful too!")

- Staying in bad relationships to avoid being alone ("He's sarcastic to me, but at least I'm not spending Saturday nights by myself!")

- Ignoring your gut feelings ("I'm not ready to sleep with him, but if I say 'no,' he'll just sleep with someone else and, besides, what's the big deal?")

It isn't always easy to see whether patterns apply to us. Let's face it—we aren't great at being objective about ourselves (this is true for the entire human race, so don't get down on yourself!). The younger you are, the less experience you have to see those patterns and to appreciate the benefits of commitment and self-protection. But, if you're not getting what you want out of dating and relationships, it can be extremely helpful to look for patterns in your dating history. Then you can learn how to change what you're doing, so you have a better chance of getting what works for you.

It's one thing to know what we want and to believe we deserve it. But often our behavior sends out an entirely different message:

- Do you want a monogamous relationship but go out with guys who are commitment-phobic?

- Do you prefer a man to make the first move but end up taking the initiative because you're afraid he won't?

- Do you like compliments and romantic gestures but date guys who are critical or unromantic?

- Do you say you want a guy who's ready to settle down, but part of you thinks those guys are less interesting than the "players"?

These are tough questions. It's a hard thing to face when familiar habits sabotage our goals. But, if you said "yes" to any of these questions, chances are your behavior is sending out a (subconscious) message that you don't feel you really deserve the kind of treatment you want.

Sometimes we're not even aware of the patterns we keep repeating. But, if we look back on our dating history, the evidence is often right there:

Emiko was dating Yoshi, who told her he wanted to be in a relationship sometime, but he had never married because he didn't want to "settle." His comment bothered Emiko, but she told herself, "He does want a relationship eventually, and meanwhile he's cute and fun." She continued to see him and disregarded her concerns. As the relationship continued, Yoshi didn't want commitment, and Emiko complained that all the good guys were taken.

Lucy had been seeing Brett for about three months when he told her he wasn't ready for a girlfriend and needed space. She was hurt—especially when she found out he was seeing someone else. Lucy decided to look for patterns in her unsuccessful relationships. She remembered that Brett was like a lot of guys she'd been attracted to—charming and flirtatious but not taking much initiative. She'd pursued them (because she'd been afraid they wouldn't make the first move), but now she realized she wanted a guy who would pursue her, even if he made a less charming first impression.

When our actions don't jibe with what we want, it's time for a little self-evaluation. Why is it so hard for us to say "no" to what we don't want? If we ignore our patterns, we keep repeating them, like Emiko's pattern of ignoring the mixed signals she got from men. But, when we look back, we can often begin to see how we're getting in our own way. Lucy had a pattern of falling for men who charmed her but didn't pursue her, so she ended up initiating more than she wanted. However, Lucy recognized her pattern and was able to change it.

How do you know whether or not to follow your gut? The more you know about yourself, the easier it will get for you to answer this question. That's why it's so helpful to look for patterns. When you notice which situations push your buttons, and how you react to them, it gives you clues to understand your motivations, and to figure out whether your GPS is sending you in the right direction. We'll talk more about this in Chapter 9.

Of course, changing patterns isn't always easy. But, once we've identified them, we can look at some of the factors that create those patterns in the first place, so we can start to make changes.

Influence: Stand Up for Yourself

Women gained power in the 1960s by banding together for change in the workplace and in the home. Today we think we have power in the dating world as well because we can ask men out and have premarital sex without stigma. But in many ways that power is an illusion—real power is knowing what works for you and having the courage to stand up for yourself. It's having the ability to say "yes" to what you want and "no" to what you don't want. You may not be there yet—and that's OK. This is a journey for all of us. But you can learn to say "no," sharpen your instincts, and develop your intuition.

If you don't care about having relationships with anyone, then maybe you can avoid learning how to stand up for yourself. Otherwise, it's a key ingredient for communication in work, play, or love. How else can we get what we want when no one else can read our minds? You already have some idea of whether this is hard for you from the exercises we did in Chapter 3 (where we discussed how hard it is to know exactly what we want, and how easy it is to be swayed by other people's opinions). Even if you don't think you have the confidence to stand up for yourself, the more you practice, the easier it will get. Remember the growth mindset approach—it's OK to be new at this.

If you're not comfortable with what a guy is doing and you let him continue, that's the hallmark of giving away your power. Of course, you have to pick your battles—I'm not talking about quibbling with his taste in clothes or not liking a restaurant he picks. But, if he does something that really bugs you, where your feelings aren't being considered, that's a sign you need to speak up. Maybe he frequently shows up 20 minutes late; maybe he pressures you to be sexual before you're ready. By drawing a clear line, you can find out whether he just doesn't know any better, whether he's testing you to see where you stand, or whether he doesn't care how you feel.

It isn't magic. When you stand up for yourself, a number of things can happen. He might develop new respect for you and begin to treat you well, or he might get mad and never call again. What matters most is that you did what was best for you, whether he liked it or not. This is the hallmark of being your own Brand of Sexy. If he disappears, you'll know he really wasn't into you. But, if he sticks around, you're in a great place to begin negotiations. Women today often put a ton of energy into figuring out how to make relationships work, but is that the best bargaining position for us? If a guy wants you, and you stand up for yourself, he'll try to find a way to make things work. (Of course, *how* you stand up for yourself is important, and we'll discuss that in Chapter 7 when we get into strategies.)

There's no need for a battle-of-the-sexes mentality. No one has to "win" or to have the last word. Isn't the best outcome some sort of dialogue where you try to understand each other and make it work? Maybe all you have to say is, "I'm not comfortable with that," and he says, "OK." Being calm and levelheaded will make it easier for him to hear what you're saying because men tune us out when they think we're being "irrational" (i.e., emotional).

Diane meets Mason at a coworker's party. They hit it off and the conversation gets flirtatious, and then Mason moves closer to her and starts to rub his hand up and down her arm. Diane just met him and isn't comfortable, but she doesn't want to come across as a prude. She's afraid if she says anything, he'll be offended or hurt.

Shantel meets Tristin at a coworker's party and he asks her to dance. The music is fairly slow, so Tristin takes Shantel in his arms and slow dances, which is fine until he slides his hand suggestively down her back. She decides to keep it light, so she takes his hand, moves it back toward him, and jokes, "Excuse me, I think this belongs to you."

Why is this so difficult for us? For starters, as we've discussed, women tend to be people-pleasers. We're conditioned to seek approval. We get messages from our culture encouraging us to be "nice girls" and to put other people's needs first. And some of us have a double whammy—it's not OK with our parents if we stand up for ourselves, leading to problems in trying to get what we want. It's scary because somebody might not like it. Let's look at these fears more closely.

What Are We So Afraid of? Conflict, Rejection, and Anger—Oh, My!

"If I say 'no,' he'll get angry. I don't want to disappoint him. What if he dumps me? I hate confrontations!" We have many fears that keep us from standing up for ourselves, and it's important to be aware of them so we can move past them. Because women are conditioned to be people-pleasers, we tend to be afraid of upsetting other people.[163] We're likely to shy away from any kind of conflict, which keeps us from standing up for ourselves. And, the more we avoid conflict, the scarier it becomes. It takes courage to face our fear but, if we start trying to stand up for ourselves, we'll get better at it with practice and ultimately become less afraid.

Hurt feelings and disappointment are simply part of the dating game that nobody can escape. But being afraid of rejection can sabotage relationships, either by making you overly sensitive or by driving you to reject him before he dumps you. How can you relax and have fun if you're always worried about being hurt?

And sometimes we don't even let ourselves get to the point of thinking about asking for what we want because it's too scary to consider even minimal conflict. For some of us, simply expressing a different opinion feels like declaring war, and we're afraid that he won't like us or we'll lose him if we disagree with him. It may seem silly to read these words, and you may not be conscious of that fear. But, if you're having trouble standing up for yourself, it's worth considering whether your fears are getting in the way. If it's too scary to disagree with a guy, then what you want goes out the window.

Fears can also lead us to accept behavior we don't like or prompt us to stay in unfulfilling, or even unhealthy, relationships. Maybe we're afraid of the unknown. If we've been seeing someone for a while, even if we're not happy, it's still scary to think about "getting back out there." And many of us are simply afraid of being alone. We think it's better to have a boyfriend than not, even if we don't like how he treats us.

When we recognize our fears, it's much easier to develop our intuition and to stand up for ourselves. How can we tell whether a guy is nice or not when we're more concerned with being rejected? Even if we're not comfortable standing up for ourselves, in the long run isn't it worse to continue being unhappy in our relationships?

Kathy has been dating Jonathan for a couple of months. He's smart and interesting, but he usually shows up 15 to 20 minutes late, blaming it on traffic. Kathy is annoyed, but the rest of the date is great so why rock the boat?

Karen has been dating Javier for a couple of months, and he also tends to run late without calling. She usually handles it with humor, joking that he's lucky she waited for him.

Karissa has been looking forward to her first date with Joe all week. She arrives at the café where they've agreed to meet on time but, after 15 minutes, Joe still hasn't shown up. She gives him a call to find out what's happened, and he says that he is running late and will be there in 20 minutes. Karissa doesn't want to have to wait another 20 minutes at the café by herself, but she feels obligated to stay. She spends the date feeling annoyed at Joe, wondering if he is really that into her, and wishing that she had let him pursue her instead of calling to track him down.

Kendall's excited about her first date with Jared until he's late and doesn't call to tell her. She's afraid of messing things up on the first date, but she doesn't want to start a relationship letting him think she will put up with this kind of treatment, so after waiting for 15 minutes she leaves. When he does show up, he can call her, and then she'll decide whether to meet him once she hears his explanation.

Nothing to Fear but Fear Itself

When we are brave enough to stand up for ourselves despite our fears, we stand a better chance of getting what we want. For starters, it reveals important information about the guy. How does he handle your discomfort? Is he angry, dismissive, or concerned that he upset you? Does he respect you for being upfront about your needs, or is he too selfish to acknowledge what you want and deserve? Some guys will disappear. Some will argue with you. Some will try to understand your point of view. Some will be critical or defensive ("You're too sensitive" or "Can't you take a joke?").

In the past, the whole idea of dating was to get to know a guy to see whether you were right for each other. Times have changed, but determining compatibility remains valuable, and standing up for what you want can speed up the process. Remember, if he disappears, he wasn't into you anyhow. If he does stick around, you'll have a better relationship when you don't expect him to read your mind. When you don't say a word about your concerns, you may end up resenting him four months later, and resentment has a nasty habit of popping out in snide comments or passive-aggressive behavior. Best of all, learning to stand up for yourself is a valuable skill in any kind of relationship.

If this seems too scary, maybe it's enough right now to simply be aware of this fear. You can try getting a little practice with standing up for yourself slowly and gradually, starting with situations where this is easier. For example, if the guy seems nice, but you aren't into him, it's probably easier to say "no" because there's less fear of losing him. If he gets angry, it's not so upsetting. If you're not quite ready for this step right now, it's OK. (If fear is a major roadblock for you, reading Chapter 9 may be helpful.)

Inner Beauty

It's a given that our society expects too much from women —just pick up any of the hundreds of books out there about how to make yourself more beautiful. We need to be thin, sexy, successful women who are able to juggle kids and a career while our homes are spotless. Models and magazine covers display unattainable outer perfection, while plastic surgery makes it appear attainable...as long as we can pay the bill. "Skin deep" beauty seems more important than inner beauty, but it is not.

Finding our inner beauty is infinitely more valuable. If we have a nose job, we may still be left with lingering insecurities about some other facet of our appearance. And, even if we are satisfied in the short term, we may continue to find new flaws in how we look over time.

Maya is a stunning, tall brunette who did some modeling in her teens. Now in her late 30s, she takes good care of her appearance. She never leaves the house without full make-up, she hits the gym five times a week, and she does regular facials and Botox, but she worries whether she should have a facelift before her looks deteriorate further. She'd like to be in a relationship, but she's convinced that she needs to lose another five pounds first.

Maya's happiness is dependent on how beautiful she thinks she is, but she is never fully satisfied. The kind of happiness that we gain when we learn to love ourselves with the extra weight, the large nose, or the big butt is deep and long-lasting. And, when we have that kind of confidence, it becomes easier to believe that someone else will love us, just the way we are.

A woman doesn't have to be "model pretty" to feel content or to radiate confidence. It may be the way she dresses, how outgoing she is, or her cheerful attitude, but she is self-assured. Women are like flowers. We are all different but each of us is beautiful in our own way.

Trish hadn't been having much luck with men, and at first she attributed that to her weight, so she started yoga class-es and nutritional counseling. She did lose a little weight, but what she really liked was the way yoga made her feel inside and out. Plus, she was making new friends and feel-ing healthier, so overall she started feeling more confident. She even went on a blind date with the cousin of one of her yoga buddies. Although she used to hate first dates, this time she was able to relax and be herself, and she ended up having a great time.

At first, Trish was focused on her appearance. But, by finding an activity that she enjoyed and making new friends, Trish found comfort and happiness within herself. She devel-oped confidence that was not dependent on how she looked, which made dating more fun. Most importantly, that kind of confidence and happiness won't fade over time. We all have the potential to be like Trish. When we're taking care of our inner *and* outer selves, when we feel confident and comfortable with who we are—that's true beauty.

"To Thine Own Self Be True"

We're pioneers at a turning point in history. It's important to realize that, if you are brave enough to face your fears and to stand up for yourself in order to gain real power, you may leave your potential romantic partners a bit confused, especially if you are opting out of the dating norm of casual sex. We can't blame guys for expecting something that's the norm. Understandably, these guys may be curious and even concerned about your decision to postpone sex. Imagine what he's thinking: "Is she very religious? Does she have a sexual problem? Is premarital sex out of the question? Is she a virgin? Does she have an STI? Is it possible that she isn't attracted to me?" He won't die of curiosity, of course, but don't be surprised if he asks you a few questions. If you think he's too shy or respectful to ask, or if you simply want to give him more information, here are some possible ways to preserve your boundaries while addressing his potential concerns:

- "I'm old-fashioned."
- "I want to get to know you better before getting more involved."
- "Casual sex doesn't work for me."
- "I'm reading this book about a new sexual revolution..."

Be your own Brand of Sexy—that means honoring who we are, how we feel, what we want, and how we stand up for ourselves. We can redefine "sexy" so that it's not just about the outside. It's about inner strength, self-knowledge, and self-confidence. If you ignore your emotions, you aren't really being true to yourself, and you're making it harder to find a relationship where your feelings matter. The more we learn to trust our intuition, the more we can truly be our own Brand of Sexy. Remember, emotional hygiene is like dental hygiene—if we take care of ourselves now, we prevent problems in the future.

Healthy self-knowledge gives us power and options—we know what we want and can treat ourselves like we deserve it. Now it's time to start looking at some strategies for achieving those goals.

7

Plan Your Strategy:
If a Guy Isn't Respecting Your Voice,
Move On

"Learn from the mistakes of others.
You can never live long enough
to make them all yourself."
—Unknown

A s modern women, must we reinvent the wheel when
it comes to dating and men? Not all old-fashioned
feminine strategies are simply relics of a bygone era.
There are some timeless truths that never go out of style.
Dating rules from the past can trigger our fears of returning
to a place we've outgrown, if not into the Middle Ages and
locked up in chastity belts, at least to the 1950s and packaged
up in girdles. But is it possible that we can honor those age-
less truths while still being true to ourselves? Believe it or not,
some of these may have value for you today, if you're open
to the idea that they might benefit you and if you consider
which could enhance your dating game plan.

Sometimes it helps to have a plan. It's much easier to stick
to a diet when you set it up in advance ("I'll have a salad
for dinner, and then those healthy snacks I prepared this
morning"). It's the same with dating—a good plan takes into
account your weaknesses. Whether you're likely to overreact

or to let him walk all over you and later feel resentful, a plan gives you a little protection. How else can you relax if you're making a lot of major decisions on your date? If you have the game plan mapped out, you can focus on enjoying yourself.

In this chapter, you'll learn how to think through some dating situations and decide ahead of time how you will respond. "But won't that kill the excitement and spontaneity?" you might be asking. I'm not advocating that you turn yourself into a robot that spits out automatic answers to questions or that is unable to adapt as situations change. I'm simply suggesting that you understand yourself well enough to know what works for you and what doesn't. This means, for example, that if last-minute invitations make you feel undervalued, this is a "rule" for you: You do not accept last-minute invitations. (Of course, if Johnny Depp calls you and invites you to the Cannes Film Festival, you might make an exception.)

If you're still not sure why it's important to stand up for yourself, this chapter will make the motivation crystal clear. Recognizing your power is the key. You might notice that most of these strategies involve facing your fears by standing up for yourself. You may not be ready to try them, or you may never want to try them, but they illustrate some basic, timeless principles that can help you improve the odds when you play the game of love.

So here is the Single Woman's 12-Piece Dating Toolbox—a variety of strategies to help you navigate the world of modern dating:

Single Woman's 12-Piece Dating Toolbox

1. Don't Drink and Date: Safety First

Making a plan is all about protecting yourself emotionally and getting treated the way that you want. This is not possible without putting your physical safety above all else.

The following protective strategies may seem obvious, but you don't want to overlook anything that might put you in danger.

Be sure you get to know a guy before you assume he's trustworthy. Just because you've exchanged 20 emails and thoroughly searched for him on the Internet doesn't mean you really know him. That's why all the Internet dating sites suggest meeting for the first time in a public place and letting a friend know where you're going. It's better to continue to meet him in public until you feel comfortable having him pick you up. You don't want somebody dangerous to have your home address. This is not being paranoid—it's just common sense. You don't want to be the one saying, "But he seemed so normal."

And don't forget what we said in Chapter 5: Alcohol and drugs affect both your inhibitions and your judgment (and can interact with any medications that you take—so read that small print you were tempted to ignore!). Remember, a few margaritas can make a frog seem like a prince. Maybe it's never happened to you, but you probably know someone who has done something under the influence that she regretted when she sobered up. Know your own tolerance so you can make decisions you can live with the next day!

> Sharon has a rule that she doesn't have sex without a con-dom, but she is a little drunk when Donny, who looks like he stepped out of an Abercrombie & Fitch ad, whispers that he'd like to take her home with him. She is caught up in the moment and has an unprotected one-night stand with hunky Donny. Although she has a great time with him, she wakes up the next day angry with herself for breaking her rule, anxious that she might contract an STI, and regretting how much she had to drink.
>
> "No condom? That's a problem!" is Sabrina's motto. She is currently dating Jack, who she has a lot of fun with. He's

gorgeous and incredibly sexy. On their third date, she's ready to have sex with him (he's been ready since day one). Things get hot and heavy and she asks him to wear a condom. Jack balks at the condom idea and says, "But I want to really feel you." Sabrina insists on the condom, and Jack gets angry, saying, "I don't need this! I don't know any other girls who make such a fuss about it." Sabrina feels like she dodged a bullet when Jack shows his true character: first-class jerk.

We've all heard of the dangers of unwanted pregnancy, STIs, and date rape. We don't need to repeat them here. But please make safety part of your dating plan. Deciding ahead of time, when you have a clear head, that you value yourself too much to take risks with your safety may save you from putting yourself in harm's way. Especially when you're faced with opposition or when your thinking is clouded by drugs, alcohol, or lust.

2. Do More by Saying Less: Actions Speak Louder Than Words

In today's culture we're used to sharing our feelings, talking things out, and being open about everything—but being completely "open and honest" often doesn't work with men. Consider the following first date:

Francisco: "I hope you like this restaurant. I've heard great things about it."

Lisa: "Yeah, I love this place. My ex-boyfriend took me here once. He broke up with me a couple of months ago, and I haven't really dated much since. The breakup was a little rough so it took me a while to get over it, but I'm glad I did. I'm having a great time!"

Notice how Lisa turned her response into a soap opera? Rehashing what went wrong in her past relationship gives the impression that Lisa isn't over her ex, and it doesn't create a positive atmosphere for a fresh start with Francisco. We all have history, but the first date isn't the time for a full disclosure of ex-boyfriends and breakups. Perhaps you can relate to saying a little more to a guy you like than you had intended to. Sometimes it's not the sheer number of words but the ones we choose to say that is the problem.

Paul calls Helen on Friday morning to ask her out for that night. Helen says, "You know, I like you, but I'd really prefer more advance notice. Do you think I just sit home and wait for you to call?" Paul had known that it was a long shot, but now he feels criticized and embarrassed. He feels like he should defend himself, but he doesn't want to have to apologize or explain when he made her a perfectly nice offer and she turned him down like that. He never calls Helen again.

Ask your male friends—how many of them relish being scolded, especially by someone they've just started dating? Yes, you want to stand up for yourself but, when you go into detail about why you're turning down the last-minute date, even if you aren't criticizing him, he's likely to feel as if you are. No one enjoys that, particularly a man who is already going out on a limb by asking you out.

Philippe calls Hannah on Friday morning to ask her out for that night. Hannah says, "I would have loved to go out, but I already have plans." She doesn't apologize or explain what her plans are, and Philippe thinks, "I wonder if she has another date or just has plans with friends." He's intrigued and decides to call sooner next time.

When Hannah said "no" gracefully, without the details, he was more likely to want to try again, thinking she's busy and popular. If you get your message across in a way that lets him save face, hopefully you'll get what you want—which is a guy who values you enough to try a bit harder!

Some women worry that, if men are aware of these dating strategies, she might come across as a woman who has studied her dating manual and is rigidly following its instructions. Being your own Brand of Sexy means figuring out what is right for you and standing up for yourself, no matter what perceptions others have.

If this approach sounds manipulative to you, consider the big picture. This is a socially acceptable way to get what you want. You are simply sticking up for what you want. You say you don't want to lie? Are you going to tell him that your hair is greasy, you're out of clean underwear, and you just sprouted a zit the size of Rhode Island on your chin? It really isn't lying to say you have plans even if your "previous commitment" consists of staying home. (Remember—less is more!) Be true to yourself and find your own comfort level with this strategy.

If what you truly want is to be desired, don't you need strategies that will maximize your chances of being pursued and of being wanted? Most strategies that protect us also serve to create pursuit if he's into you and keep him away if he's not. Either way, it works.

3. Turn Down What You Don't Want With Grace and Dignity: I'm Just a Girl Who CAN Say "No"

How you say "no" to what you don't want (for example, a premature sexual advance) is important. You're simply standing up for yourself and setting your boundaries. You are essentially saying, "This is what is best for me; this is not how I want to be treated."

Rick asks Melanie out for dinner and dancing and suggests they meet halfway, which is a half-hour drive from her house. She really isn't comfortable driving in rush-hour traffic, but she wants to go out with him and is afraid he won't ask again if she turns him down, so she agrees. She doesn't tell Rick that she got lost following his directions and that she's stressed by the situation, so she can't relax and feels flustered. Rick can tell something is wrong, but assumes she is standoffish or not interested.

Obviously the passive approach doesn't get Melanie anywhere. What if she had just said, "I'm not comfortable driving in rush hour" when Rick asked her? Either Rick would honor that or he would show that he really didn't care about her enough to drive across town and pick her up.

Saying "no" can be awkward, so it's easier on both of you to soften the blow. Be nice.

Here's the formula: You smile so he knows you like him (he can hear it in your voice over the phone) and you express some enthusiasm about his idea or being with him, and combine it with your "no." And your "no" is all about how you feel. Use "I" language: "I'm not comfortable, I'm not ready." ("Hiking is a great idea, but I'd feel more comfortable meeting in a public place until I know you better.") How can anybody argue with how you feel? He can disagree or even dump you, but it's pretty hard to argue with someone's feelings. If he says, "Why?," all you have to do is to repeat yourself, "I'm just not comfortable. It just doesn't feel right." It's OK if he asks you for an explanation, but it's a big red flag if he asks you repeatedly to explain your discomfort. If he's into you at all, he probably cares how you feel and doesn't want you to feel uncomfortable. If he's not into you, he'll be history very soon anyway.

This ability to say "no" isn't just important to dating; it's important to every relationship you have. If you want a relationship with a man, how will you ever make it work if you can't stand up for yourself? Will you be happy if it's all his way? It takes practice, particularly if you're not used to saying "no," or if your normal strategy is to pour out your feelings and discuss things to death. It might also help to view standing up for yourself as a collaboration (you both benefit if he knows what you want) rather than as a confrontation (where there are accusations and recriminations). Start small—turn down a last-minute date from someone you're not that interested in, so it doesn't feel so risky.

Remember, you're more likely to get what you want if saying "no" to what you *don't* want is part of your plan.

4. Don't Make Yourself Readily Available: Find Out If Absence Makes His Heart Grow Fonder, or If You Are "Out of Sight, Out of Mind"

In the movie *When Harry Met Sally*, Harry and Sally are "just friends."[164] But when her ex calls to say he's getting married, Sally calls Harry to come over to comfort her. One thing leads to another, and "Uh-oh!" They end up in bed. Harry thinks it was a mistake and wants their relationship to return to the "friends" stage. But Sally—needing to protect herself—disappears from his life, telling him she can no longer be his consolation prize. Harry didn't realize how he felt about Sally until he was forced to live without her. (Imagine what would have happened if Sally had agreed to be "just friends," as so many of us do.)

A breakup is a drastic example of creating enough space in a relationship to allow a guy to recognize his feelings. Wouldn't you prefer to create this space without the misery of a breakup? Let's explore the nuances with an example, using the strategy of playing the field, which we'll discuss more later. Not only does this strategy ensure that you're too busy dating several men to obsess about one, you're also creating a dynamic that lets him worry about the possibility of losing you. Men often need space to realize how they feel about a woman. How can they possibly miss us when we're calling, texting, and asking what plans they have for the weekend before they've even thought about asking us?

> Naomi and Greg have been dating for over a year. They get along well and she really wants to get married, but his foot-dragging makes her wonder if he's really the one. So she continues to see him occasionally but makes other plans, seeing friends and taking a class. At first he just teases her about her busy life, but eventually he sees how much he misses her when they're apart. He starts trying to see her more often, planning nice dates when they do see each other, and sending her flowers and romantic texts. The more effort he makes, the stronger Naomi's feelings grow, and they end up feeling ready to get married.

In the past women had strategies that were geared toward giving men this space. For example, women were supposed to wait for men to call. These days, advances in technology have given us a myriad of new ways to smother men. If you call and text them, they often think, "Oh, no. She's too into me." They feel they don't deserve this devotion. And they may take a step back. (But they may have casual sex with you first!) If you move closer still, they move farther away. In fact, they may move to another ZIP code and change their phone number. If you complain they aren't calling, you've compounded the problem by nagging, which feels (to them) like you're criticizing. When you're the one doing the chasing, can you still feel desired and pursued?

> Jennie and Roger hit it off the second they meet, and they can't get enough of each other. They're together almost every night, and call and text each other all the time. After a few dates, they get sexually involved. Then things cool down a bit. He's not calling or texting as much, and they don't get together as often. Concerned with the change in

their relationship, Jennie asks Roger if there is a problem. He says everything is fine, he's just gotten busy at work, but Jennie is still worried. She's calling and texting him every day, complaining when he doesn't get back to her as soon as she'd like. He starts to get annoyed and tells her he's got to get his work done.

When things cool off, are you the one doing most of the texting or calling? If anyone suggests that you pull back a little to let the guy breathe, do you think, "I don't want to play games"? It isn't a game to give someone breathing room; it's actually a way for you to show that you respect his commitments and the rest of his life.

It's harder to cut our losses when we've invested a lot of time and energy into a losing proposition. When we gamble with our hearts, like other forms of gambling, we can throw away good money in order to justify how much we've already invested. Instead of facing the idea that we made a mistake, we want to fix the situation, so we take even more risks. We cling to the guy who told us he loved us, even when he's no longer calling very often. But then how do you know whether he's truly into you? Is he just responding to your efforts or are his feelings really growing? Often it's hard to know what's real unless you give him some space.

But it's hard to let go when you're bonded. And, for at least some of us, sex probably makes that bond stronger, so it's even harder to let go. I'm not suggesting you drop off the planet, only that you give him the space to miss you and to let him call you.

Many women worry that this strategy will give the wrong impression, causing the man to assume that they just aren't interested and to give up the chase. So let's get into the finer points of how to pull this off. You want to strike a balance between "head over heels" and "forget it." Ideally, you genuinely feel this way since (if you haven't known him very long) you can't really know yet where you stand. You're interested in getting to know him better but not sold yet. The attitude is a playful "convince me."

It helps to know what your behavior is like with men. Are you flirty or needy, so that you become obvious when you really like someone? Or are you shy and reserved, or maybe a little nervous or afraid of them? If you're the former, you may want to tone yourself down a bit so you don't go overboard and prematurely tell him that he's the greatest guy you ever met or you're ready to move in. But, if you're a little distant with men, you may want to warm up those interactions. Here are some possible statements to use—the difference is in the delivery. Practice saying these with a big smile if you're reserved, and be careful not to jump the gun if you're drooling all over him.

- "It's nice to see you again."
  (Stop before saying, "It's been too long!")

- "It's nice to hear from you."
  (Stop before saying, "Why haven't you called?")

- "Oh, no! Unfortunately, I have other plans."
  (Don't say, "But I'll rearrange them!")

Just because you're a little hard to get doesn't mean you can't let him know that you're enjoying yourself. This helps with the head-over-heals/forget-it balance and has other benefits we'll discuss in the section below.

- "The moon looks so beautiful tonight!"

- "What a delicious meal!"

- "That's really interesting!"

- "That's so sweet!" (if he compliments you)

"Playing hard to get" is the classic strategy that many of us believe is passé. But it's often quite effective. What other strategy protects you, makes you more alluring (or weeds out men who aren't into you), and gives a guy the space to recognize how he feels? It slows down the pace of the relationship, so you have time to figure out whether or not he's a good bet. Of course, as we saw above, it's better to *be* hard to get rather than *play* hard to get. If you're busy with your life, you naturally won't be able to answer whenever he calls or be able to go out whenever he suggests. Nobody's recommending that you be impossible to get—that's too discouraging. Just don't answer all his questions or do whatever he wants all the time. Have your own opinions. Have your own life!

5. Let Him Lead: Shall We Dance?
A Metaphor for Dating

In our desire to prove that we are strong and independent and can carry our own luggage, we may be robbing men of something they love to do—the opportunity to make us happy. Think about it: The more powerful women become, the more useless men can feel. What could be wrong with giving them a chance to make us happy?

Imagine what it's like on the dance floor when you try to lead. Dating is like dancing, the old-fashioned way. If you've ever taken ballroom dancing lessons, or watched it on TV, you probably know the basics of partner dancing: The man leads, the woman follows. He's in charge of deciding which way to go, how to get there, and how to avoid crashing into other couples. I know, that sounds so retro—but letting him lead doesn't rob you of your power. The French have a saying, "*L'homme propose et la femme dispose*," which means the man makes suggestions, and the woman decides the outcome. Even if you let him lead, this doesn't mean you are passive—

you are the decision maker. This is a timeless strategy that has the potential to create enough space to make his heart grow fonder.

Today we ask men to "dance" (both on the dance floor and in the dating world), which often puts us at a disadvantage. Even a modern man will often think, "What's wrong with her if she's pursuing me—is she desperate? Does she want to hook up?" It may be the 21st century, but many men still find a woman more desirable if she's not so easily available.

> At a business event, Chloe meets Mitchell. They hit it off, and he gives her his card. She's a modern woman who has no problem with calling him; he sounds glad to hear from her and suggests a restaurant where they can meet. They agree to split the check and he seems to have a good time. He's affectionate and flirtatious, but after the date she doesn't hear from him. What happened? Should she call again? She thought she did enough to get things started, but is he waiting for her to pursue him some more, or is he just not that into her despite how he behaved on the date?

What happened with Chloe and Mitchell? Some women are the initiators, leaders, and decision makers in their relationships—and it works for them. The problem arises for many of us when we're leading and it doesn't work. Some of us can come on too strong. We're taught that we have to be assertive to get ahead at work, so many of us carry assertiveness into our dating lives as well. If you're like Chloe and want to feel sought after (he calls, plans the date, and treats you), it may not work for you when you're the one doing the pursing (you initiate, you plan the date). Do you feel as special when you're the one calling him? Of course, if you truly prefer leading, you'll find men who are comfortable with you taking the initiative, but you may have to be patient and risk some rejection. Or they may simply be looking for casual sex and assume that's what you want.

Equality is important to us. We want men to respect our opinions, and many men want to please us by treating us as equal partners in decision-making. And, if we start to take control, men may relinquish the lead to us because they want to please us. But, if you ask him out, do you feel desired? If you're always helping him with directions or telling him where to go, do you start to feel like his mother? (That's not likely to be a turn-on for either of you.) When we take the lead, we can lose the signals that women used in the past to tell whether men are into us or not.

Imagine how the man feels. He's trying hard to impress with his ability to provide by planning a nice date or opening doors and showing he's competent at being in charge. If he feels responsible for leading, our attempts to lead can push against his, and it may feel confusing to him, like we're fighting him. Equality is fabulous, but dancing can be hard with two people in charge.

> David and Farah have gone out several times. He offers to take her out for dinner and asks where she'd like to go. She suggests a few places she knows, but he doesn't like them or has heard negative reviews. He keeps asking her for more suggestions until she feels uncomfortable. Finally she says, "You always pick nice places, why don't you decide?" He takes her to a new place that they both love, and she says, "You're so good at finding wonderful restaurants. I like that about you." He thinks, "Wow, Farah is nice and she has great taste!"

When a man takes the initiative, he might be saying, "Your feelings matter; I want to make you happy; stay with me and I'll take good care of you." So when you complain that he's opened your door ("I'm a capable, independent woman") or you'd rather go to a different nightclub ("That place is so over-rated!"), he might get the sense that he can't make you happy. There are softer ways to express yourself that are less likely to feel critical to him. If you explain why you're not comfortable, and ask him to solve the problem, you're still letting him feel like a man. "How sexist," you might think. We're not just talking about gender roles, we're talking about how he feels. There's nothing wrong with rewarding the behavior you want with charm and compliments. Give him a sign that you like what he's doing. If you're having a good time, he's more likely to feel like he can make you happy.

- "It's fun dancing with you!"
- "Your mother raised a real gentleman."
- "The stars are so beautiful tonight!"
- "What a good story!"
- "How nice. I really appreciate that!" (if he opens your door or does anything nice for you)

If you let him lead, you give him the chance to make you happy—and you have the chance to see if he can actually do it. If you're pleased and let him know you appreciate his efforts, he feels like a hero. This is what it means to "woo" and to court a woman, to earn her favor by treating her well.

6. Prune the Good Guys and Get Rid of the Weeds: Guard-ening Your Heart

You *might* be able to shape a man's behavior, if he's into you— maybe. Many of us possess the dangerous belief that we can change a man, but it's more like pruning a shrub in your garden. You might be able to shape his behavior a little, but you can't change his basic nature. Being your own Brand of Sexy is doing what's best for you, whether or not the man changes. Don't expect to change him completely but, if he cares about your feelings, he might change a little. And if he doesn't show any willingness to bend, you have a clear signal that either he's not that interested or he's so set in his ways that he's a lost cause.

Don and Melinda have been dating for a year. She hears wedding bells and they have casual conversations about getting married, but they are not engaged. Unexpectedly, Don gets a job offer across the country and asks Melinda to relocate with him. Melinda agonizes over her decision. Moving means leaving the family, friends, and job she dearly loves. She loves Don but doesn't want to move. She realizes that she isn't comfortable leaving without a bigger commitment from Don or without knowing that they are at least on the same page about the future. She decides that she'd rather risk ending the relationship than go along silently with a situation that makes her uncomfortable, so she tells him how she feels. Don is resistant to marriage, so he suggests they try a long-distance relationship and see how it goes. Melinda says that won't work for her, and they go their separate ways. She is sad to break up but knows she did the right thing by listening to her gut rather than staying with a guy who doesn't want the same thing as her.

Melinda said "no" to what she didn't want, and then gave him the space to decide what he wanted. She made the decision to tell Don about her discomfort with the situation knowing that he may not have reacted positively, but she realized that the only way to determine if they were on the same page was to be honest about her feelings and needs. Standing your ground can be hard especially if you risk losing the guy but, if he's not willing to listen to your feelings or compromise, he may not be the right guy for you.

Here are some ways to practice your pruning skills:

- If he wants you to go out the night you meet: "I'd love to but I have an early day tomorrow."

- If he gives you his card and asks you to call him: "I'd love to talk sometime, but I don't call men."

- If he invites you to come to his place sooner than you're ready: "I'd love to get together, but I'm not comfortable going to your place."

If he likes you, he won't let these little roadblocks stop him. If he doesn't, that may be the end of him. Of course, sometimes the problem requires more than a little pruning—some guys simply won't catch on. If a guy is oblivious to your needs, if you've tried pruning and he still expects you to meet him halfway, you can just keep saying "no." He'll weed himself out.

Saying "no" to what you don't want makes it easier to weed out the men who aren't that into you, leaving the guys who are. If you don't weed your garden, what happens? Those weeds can take over and steal all the nutrients, so flowers don't grow as well. With dating, if you go out with a lot of guys who don't treat you well, it can drain your energy and lower your self-confidence. Isn't it stressful to spend time with somebody who doesn't hear you or doesn't really care how you feel?

Remember, it all depends on the man. There is no magic formula to change a guy who isn't into you. The only magic involved is the certainty that if he's only interested in what he wants, and you refuse, you might as well have waved your magic wand because he's going to disappear. We're frequently disappointed when men disappear, but perhaps we should feel grateful when they weed themselves out.

After dating for six months, Bryan and Beth have established a pattern. He tells dirty jokes in front of their friends even though she has asked him not to. When she complains about it, he tells her to grow up and stop being so sensitive. Beth is tired of his behavior, but she has let him get away with it for so long, she has given up on reforming him. She decides to confront him one last time. "Bryan, I'm embarrassed when you tell dirty jokes in front of me.

It's demeaning and I'm tired of you dismissing my feelings about it. Would you please stop?" He looks at her in surprise and says, "Are you kidding me? That's just who I am. You knew that from the beginning." Beth decides that Bryan will never respect her feelings and she breaks it off.

Like Beth, it's good to know what types of behavior are "deal breakers" for you. Some women even make a list. These are things that you can't or won't tolerate (everyone is different—this list is personal).

Would these be deal breakers for you or just make you proceed with caution?

- You're asked out by a man who's married but separated.

- He threatens to break up with you if you won't have sex.

- He takes you out for dinner and treats the waitress in a very condescending and disparaging manner.

- You're at a party together and he spends the whole evening flirting with a very attractive woman he just met.

- On your second date, he asks if you have any Vicodin in your purse.

- The "morning after," instead of sending flowers, he texts you a photo of his penis.

Would these behaviors make you reach for the weed whacker? It's worth taking the time to make your own list as part of your dating plan.

It must be said, though, that a list of unacceptable behaviors is not the same as the list many single women keep—the one that looks like this: Must be over 6' tall, have blue eyes, work out every day, make more than $100,000 a year, have no children or pets, and (oh, yeah) have a degree from Harvard or Yale.

Women who are happily married often tell me that their husband met few (or even none) of the criteria they had mapped out, but they were won over by his kindness and sense of humor. So don't be too restrictive in your thinking about what your dream man should look like or do for a living. *Do* decide how you want to be treated and stick to it.

The bottom line: You can prune now or later when faced with these types of obstacles. It's your choice when to have the pain and heartbreak. (Be honest. How many times have you heard of a relationship with a married man working out without any drama?) If you express your reluctance, he can disappear or work harder to make the situation better. It's up to him to show you whether he's a destructive weed or a nice shrub who just needs a little pruning.

Now, imagine that enough women are doing this "pruning" maneuver that men in general start to get the point. We might be able to train a whole generation of men to treat us better. Hooray for sisterhood!

7. Play the Field: After You've Weeded It!

Serial monogamy works when your instincts and intuition are good. But, if your instincts are not reliable, or you don't take the time to evaluate the guy, you're taking yourself off the market for a roll of the dice. Don't forget how hard frequent breakups can be emotionally and physiologically.

In the old days, one of the advantages of virginity was that it kept your options open. Playing the field meant you could date as many men as you wanted, maximizing your chances of marrying. These men didn't wonder if you were having sex with anybody else. If you weren't getting close to sex with them, they were fairly sure you weren't having sex with other men. Today you can play the field, but men may assume you're sleeping with other guys too if you sleep with them without an understanding of monogamy. Yes, it's the 21st century, but how many men do you know who want their *love* interest to have sex with other men? Of course, they don't mind if you're just "for sex," but is that what you want to be to him? The object of playing the field is to find a good man who wants to be committed—to you.

Playing the field protects you. It is harder for you to get hung up on any one man when you're busy dating several others. If you're only dating one, it's a much shorter drive to Obsessionland. And, if you're obsessed with a guy, it can be harder to say "no" to him because you're likely to be afraid of losing him. Playing the field also gives you time to evaluate whether he's a good bet. Many men want sex quickly but will wait if they're into you.

Holding back leads to heightened anticipation and allows time for courtship—which makes him feel he deserves you, and makes you feel more desired. When he feels he deserves you and had to work to get you, he tries harder than a guy who didn't have to work very hard—you know, the one who is more likely to take you for granted.

Dating a variety of men also gives him the space to figure out how much he wants you and the opportunity to chase you. Now some may accuse you of manipulation if you don't have sex with him in the hope of getting the commitment you want. But why shouldn't it be OK for you to wait for the kind of relationship you want or at least an arrangement you can live with? By waiting for monogamy, you can weed out the guys who only want something casual and find the ones who are looking for the same thing you are—a committed relationship.

Kailani goes on dates with several different men. She likes them all for various reasons, but she's not sure whether any of them is "Mr. Right," so she keeps it casual and uses the time to get to know more about each of them. Meanwhile, a few of the guys really like her, and wondering if they have competition motivates them to step up their game. They put more effort into taking her on nice dates, and she gets to know them even better. Kailani enjoys the attention and doesn't feel the pressure to commit to one guy. She appreciates having choices. Eventually, she feels the strongest connection to Jeff and he asks her to be monogamous and build their relationship. She feels good that "Mr. Right" stepped up and won her over.

Right now you may be thinking, "I don't know where this Kailani person lives, but I'm lucky to find *one* single guy worth dating, let alone a group of them!" If the opportunity to date several guys doesn't present itself, just make sure that the one you're dating doesn't become too important before you get to know him. Don't build your life around someone you barely know—make sure your life is full of other friends and interests.

8. Be Patient: Anything Really Good Is Worth Waiting For

If you have been dating for any time at all, it will be no surprise to you that some guys sometimes try to manipulate women. They think, "If I can get an inch, she may give me a mile." Do any of the following lines sound familiar?

- "Can I spend the night on your couch? It's a long drive home."

- "Let's sleep together. I promise no funny stuff."

- "I just want to snuggle."

- "You led me on, and now I'll get blue balls!"

153

If you want to play the field, it's important to be able to say "no" earlier to behaviors that get you close to sex. Otherwise, it can be a slippery slope once you get started.

- "I always enjoy being with you, but... I'm not ready for dinner at your place."

- "I'm attracted to you, but...I don't know you well enough to have sex."

- "I wish it wasn't so late, but...I've got a big day tomorrow and have to get up early."

- "I like snuggling, but...I'm just not comfortable with that yet."

What if he simply can't wait long enough for you to get to know him as well as you'd like? Then you know he's not that into you. A guy who's into you will wait, even if it's not his first choice.

After only a few dates, Jeremy asks Lynn if he can spend the night. She tells him she's not ready for sex, and he pleads with her, saying, "But I want you so badly—we have a special connection, and you're the only woman for me!" Lynn tells him she's flattered but she still wants to wait. Two weeks go by, and she doesn't hear from him, but she finds out he's sleeping with someone else. So much for being "the only woman for him"!

After only a few dates, Jaxon asks Linda if he can spend the night. She tells him she's not ready for sex, and he pleads with her, saying, "I really like you, and I want to make love to you." Linda tells him she's flattered but she still wants to wait. Jaxon isn't happy about her decision, but he likes her enough to be willing to wait. They continue dating and, by the time they do have sex, they've gotten to know each other really well. Linda knows he's a nice guy, so she feels much safer and doesn't feel like she's gambling with her heart.

Patience also helps when you're getting to know a man. We can appear desperate or pushy when we're simply trying to avoid another broken heart by finding out as much as we can right away. Sometimes men feel grilled by our questions. It can seem more like a job interview than a date. Believe it or not, you can get answers to your questions without asking him directly if you listen and pay attention to what he says.

What's the hurry to get all those answers anyway? Aren't you more likely to have a future date if you make this one as pleasant as possible? If he's relaxed, he might open up more. And (this may shock you) men don't always tell the truth. Maybe he's not comfortable being brutally honest with you right away, or maybe he's a lying cad—it takes time to tell the difference.

Some women like asking questions that get right to the point about whether he wants marriage or why his last relationship didn't work out. They feel they're wasting their time if they don't find out immediately where the guy stands. Sometimes later on in a relationship it's important to find out if he is on the same page about the future, as we saw with Don and Melinda, but early in a relationship this technique can be risky. Plenty of men want marriage to be their idea when they meet the right woman and don't like the idea of having to prove how serious they are about it. Just because he doesn't like it if you bring up marriage right away doesn't always mean he's not marriage material. This might be another area where it's possible the man wants to lead, but you are taking the lead away from him. And guess what? He may believe he's giving you truthful answers, but they aren't necessarily the truth. Just because he says he's ready for marriage doesn't mean he's capable of committing. Actions speak louder than words. Sure, listen to what he tells you, but don't forget to notice whether what he's doing matches what he says.

Whatever requirements are on your checklist of qualities you are looking for in a guy, when you place those items above the importance of enjoying his company and appreciating his efforts, something is not going to feel right. Nobody likes to be put on the spot.

The other benefit of taking your time is that you give the man time to decide and to make the next move. If you want pursuit and desire, depending on the man, you may have to wait, be patient, and let him be in charge sometimes. Meanwhile, you can be exploring other options. If he doesn't pursue you, you can cut your losses easily and find someone who is truly interested. We're so afraid to be passive or submissive because so many of women's problems in the past stemmed from a culture that enforced female passivity. We are afraid that being passive will encourage those past beliefs that we *should* be passive. But letting a man pursue you isn't necessarily passive, as long as you're not sitting at home waiting for his call, putting your life on hold.

Sometimes the man needs a bit of time to realize he can't live without you. Don't forget Elizabeth Bennet's sister Jane, in *Pride and Prejudice.*[165] She went to London in the hopes of seeing Mr. Bingley, who'd disappeared from her life. Alas, it was to no avail because Bingley wasn't ready to see her. But never fear—when Bingley finally came back to Jane's neighborhood, it was to propose! We can't always control our relationships. That hasn't changed in all these years. The man needs to be ready just like you have to be ready. But we don't have to merely wait. Jane Bennet was free to have other suitors, and so are you.

> Melissa has been dating Sam for several months. He tells her he's not ready for a commitment so they should both see other people. She says she's fine with that and starts accepting other dates. Sam starts getting jealous of the other men and tells Melissa he loves her and that he's ready

for a commitment as long as she doesn't expect a ring. She agrees to be monogamous but continues her other activities, and he realizes how much he misses her when they're not together. Meanwhile, a couple of his friends have gotten married, so he realizes it isn't so scary. He wants to be with Melissa and decides he's ready to propose.

Whether it's waiting to have sex, waiting for a commitment, or waiting for a good man to come along, patience can be very difficult. At least time is usually on your side when you're protecting yourself emotionally because absence will either make his heart grow fonder, or he'll become a footnote in the history book of your dating life.

9. Keep a Few Things to Yourself: Don't Show All Your Cards at Once

Privacy can be a refreshing antidote to our modern-day tendency of letting it all hang out. But we each have different sensibilities when it comes to privacy and personal questions.

What's your comfort level with personal questions? Often, when men ask us personal questions, we feel obligated to answer, despite our discomfort ("What happened to your last relationship? How old are you?"). You can always just ignore the question, or you can avoid answering directly by responding with one of the following:

- "Why do you ask?"

- "Sorry, classified info."

- "I'm old enough to know I don't have to answer that."

- "My ex is a great guy—it just didn't work out."

- "My, you ask personal questions!"

- "You've got to be kidding."

And then there's the big question, the one that you not only get asked by men but also at every wedding (and every blind date and every family get-together): "Why aren't you married?" Pick an answer that suits your personality and the occasion:

- "I was too smart to get married."
- "It gives my mother something to live for."
- "I already have enough laundry to do, thank you."
- (Sigh) "Ah, so many men, so little time!"
- "Why must I do everything that's trendy?"

Now, some questions are fair game. If he wants kids and you can't have them, you're wasting his time if he asks you and you don't let him know that bearing his kids isn't in the cards. But it doesn't mean you have to give him every gory detail of your fertility problems. And please don't tell him all about your last breakup or your troubles with depression and anxiety when you're just getting to know him.

Even if he doesn't ask personal questions, many of us have a tendency to want to spill our guts on the first date. After all, "I'm just being myself. Isn't it important to be honest?" Sure, but how many guys do you think will ask you out again if you spend the first date going on about the ex-boyfriend who still owes you money or giving him the play-by-play of all your issues with your mother? It's OK not to reveal all your cards at the beginning. Until you've taken the time to get to know him, you may not want to reveal everything about yourself. Remember, if he's interested, he'll welcome the opportunity to get to know you better.

Many men want what doesn't come easily, and they feel like the trophy isn't as valuable if they didn't work hard to earn it. It's human nature. Maybe it's true that we've spoiled men by making "the chase" easy for them, so some of them don't feel like they have to work that hard, especially if they're good-looking and/or wealthy (you know who they are). But, if you remain more mysterious and elusive, it just might motivate them to work a little harder to pursue you. At the very least, it will sort out the men from the boys.

10. Figure Out What He's Really Like: Does He Have Character or Is He Actually Just a "Character"?

Character matters. Some of us are so hungry for a relationship that we ignore the warning signs. But, if he's behaving badly now, realize this is only the beginning! Courtship is a snapshot of your future relationship. He may be hot, but do you want to be trapped in a relationship with a guy whose immaturity or inconsideration will become a problem for you? Wouldn't your life be more enhanced by a man who's grown up and responsible and who values your feelings?

> Laura has a history of dating irresponsible, charming, artsy types—actors and musicians who expect her to split the bill at even the cheapest diners. So when she meets Bill, he sweeps her off her feet. He makes good money, he initiates and plans lovely dates (for which he insists on paying), and he even helps her when her car gets towed. She appreciates the contrast with her other dates, but she's not crazy about the way he makes sarcastic remarks all the time, putting her down for being disorganized and criticizing her appearance. Laura realizes that, while Bill is good at making the grand gestures, his real character is revealed by how he treats her in private.

Learning more about his character protects you from disappointment and helps you figure out if he's relationship material. Nice guys complain about our love of the bad boys, saying we find nice guys too boring. Do these relationships with the bad boys lead to anything more than a hookup or a crash-and-burn kind of relationship?

On the first few dates, all you have to do to assess his character is pay attention. Guys are usually on their best behavior. Try to have fun, and be a good companion. Always find something to appreciate about your date. And, if you notice a guy doing something sweet and thoughtful, strong and brave, or intelligent—tell him how much you appreciate it. (Everyone loves to be thanked, and a guy whose efforts get acknowledged will feel like a superhero as well as being more likely to continue doing the things you liked.)

Another good reason to let a man help you is to assess his character. A man who wants to help you put on your coat is more likely to be more considerate months into the relationship than the man who doesn't even ask you which wine you prefer. There is nothing wrong with wanting the modern-day version of a little old-fashioned courtship. Today men can still slay dragons for us in order to win our hearts, although it may take the form of fixing our computers or making us dinner.

You may be thinking, "Wait a minute! First she tells me to be independent and have my own life, and then she tells me to ask guys for help. Which is it?" I'm not suggesting that you pretend to be needy or incompetent. Women worry that wanting help from a man is some fatal flaw, but you aren't hiding your competence when you're a woman with a good job who could use a little help with moving furniture. Independent, self-sufficient women and men still need help now and then. How can you assess how willing he is to help you if you insist on being completely self-sufficient? If you ask for a little help, it won't interfere with your ability to find out if he is threatened by your self-sufficiency.

You can also get a lot of helpful hints from his behavior in general. For example:

- His actions speak louder than his words.
  (He says, "Take your time ordering," but he's rolling his eyes and checking his watch.)

- His words are important too. (Yes, he may change his mind for a woman as wonderful as you but, if he says he never wants to get married, be careful!)

- His apologies are half-hearted or he throws the blame back on you. ("I'm sorry you're upset, but I think you're overreacting.")

- He takes care of things (plans dates, helps you hook up your printer) but is condescending or demeaning.

Watch out for the obvious red flags, like drinking heavily, flirting with other women, and making critical remarks—no matter how cute or appealing he is, those behaviors are likely to get worse. And, if you run into logistics issues, like crazy work schedules or distance, see if he's willing to work to find a solution. (If you think "love conquers all," you might ignore obstacles and give him no incentive to try to solve the problem.) If you ask, "What can we do about this?" you're asking him to figure it out and seeing if he will.

11. Think Ahead: Every Star Needs a Script and an Entourage

When you know how you will handle a situation, you don't face a major decision every minute of your interactions with men, so you can relax and have fun. Your plan lets you feel protected. And you can always decide to change it later if something isn't working for you.

Planning your strategy before the date increases the likelihood that you'll succeed in making the kinds of changes we've discussed. It's much easier to stick to new resolutions (delaying sex, not revealing too much too soon) if you've rehearsed your lines in advance, so you can get comfortable saying, "I'm not comfortable with that." And it makes it less likely that you'll give in to last-minute temptation ("He's so cute. Do I really want to wait?").

Gina and her friend Bonnie spend many lunch hours re-hashing disastrous dates. The phrase "What I should have said was…" is used a lot. Gina decides she wants to stop making the same mistakes and enlists Bonnie's help in role-playing dating situations. They practice saying "no" politely, staying in control of a situation, and discouraging unwanted behavior. When Gina goes on a date and the guy asks her why she's never been married, instead of recounting her entire dating history as she would have in the past, she says simply, "I'm waiting for the stars to be properly aligned," just the way she and Bonnie had rehearsed.

It's difficult to change your behavior without some support. Having somebody to keep you accountable is an important key to making all this work. If you're the only one who's keeping yourself honest, you might overlook a few blind spots. It's a little like dieting or getting fit. It's much easier to resist the conference-room donuts or to exercise when you commit to telling a friend what you ate, or to meeting her at the gym. Likewise, if you promise a friend you won't give in and accept a last-minute date like you usually do, it's easier to stick to that resolution. Left to our own devices, we may fall into our old patterns.

But you can't just pick anyone. Make sure you rely on someone who you know will support both your goals *and* your plan to reach them. You don't want your support system to question your strategy midway. You want someone to keep you honest and be supportive if you get off track.

12. Be Honest With Yourself: Nothing Will Work If You Aren't

Perhaps the most important tool of all is to be honest with yourself about your needs, wants, and emotions. Sometimes we focus so much on who we think we should be, or who we want to be, that we forget who we really are. But, in order to attract a compatible partner and build a healthy relationship, you have to be honest with yourself.

Carla goes on lots of dates that usually end up in bed. Deep down she wants to be in a committed relationship but figures that she might as well have fun until she finds the right guy for her. She is always nervous about the sex, but chalks it up to first-date nerves and tells herself that as long as she uses a condom there's not much risk. Afterward she always goes home feeling disappointed and wondering when she will meet someone whom she can settle down with.

Carla isn't being honest with herself. Instead, she's convinced herself that casual sex works for her, even though it doesn't make her happy. If Carla were honest with herself about her discomfort with casual sex, her unsuccessful dating strategy, and her need to protect herself emotionally, she could approach dating differently and in a way that was a lot more fun and a lot less disappointing.

Carla might start by asking herself the following questions: "Is there another reason I'm nervous about the sex? If I end up disappointed, why do I keep doing this? Is it possible that casual sex isn't right for me?"

Being honest with yourself can be difficult. It can require you to make decisions that go against the crowd, and it can force you into seeing parts of yourself that you'd rather ignore. Try confiding in a close friend or therapist, or writing your truths down in a journal and reminding yourself of them before dates ("Casual sex doesn't work for me" or "More than two glasses of wine and I'm toast"). This may help you to stay honest with yourself during the date and to make healthy decisions. Once you understand and accept who you are and what you need, you put yourself on the path toward getting what you want.

Using Your Toolbox:
Making These Strategies Work for You

Where are you in this process? Are you ready to start saying "no" to some things, or are you still trying to figure out what you need to change and where to start?

When you plan your strategy, take into account that change is often harder than it seems. Those old ways are familiar and comfortable. It's always best to have realistic expectations of how much you can change in a short period of time. If you can set your expectations low, success is easier to achieve, giving you the confidence to attempt more change. Otherwise, you could be setting yourself up for failure. Expect a few setbacks, and try to handle them with a growth mindset (the point of view that says, "I still need some practice"). Celebrate your progress. Many of us focus on what we could do better rather than the progress we've made. Progress, no matter how small, is moving in the direction you want. Enjoy it. And remember, you need a little intuition and the ability to stand up for yourself (so, if you skipped the last chapter, this might be a good time to go back and read it).

Some truths are timeless. Since we were expected to conform to these rules in the past, we rebelled and trashed them, even though they still have value to help us protect ourselves and to create successful relationships. Today we can pick and choose which of these tools feels useful to us as individuals. Doing more and saying less, saying "no" gracefully, weeding out undesirable behavior, retaining some distance and mystery, and being willing to wait can protect women from guys who aren't that into them—and can create the space for the guys who could be into them. Wisdom is timeless, not trendy. And, as we'll see in the next chapter, there are lots of different ways to use these tools. Remember, being your own Brand of Sexy is about doing what works best for you!

8

Script Your New Game: A Dating Quiz

*"No trumpets sound when
the important decisions of our life are made.
Destiny is made known silently."*[166]
—Agnes de Mille

A s we've seen in earlier chapters, change begins with awareness. The following quiz illustrates a range of possible responses to some common pitfalls in dating. As you read them, see if you recognize yourself in any of the examples. You might even see yourself in more than one response. Keep track of your responses to get an assessment of your patterns at the end.

You'll get much more out of this chapter if you're willing to be honest with yourself—there are no right or wrong answers, and you don't have to share your responses with anyone else. Perhaps make two lists: one for how you have handled these situations in the recent past, and another for how you would like to handle them in the future. Focus on how you'd feel if you were in that situation and which response would feel better to you.

Noncommittal Ned:
Do you put your life on hold when you wait for a man?

A man you would love to go out with asks, "What are you doing this weekend?" You tell him you're open, and he says, "I'll call you," but doesn't mention a specific time. He calls you Thursday to ask you out Friday.

a. You've kept your weekend open just in case he called, so you eagerly accept the last-minute invite.

b. You're really annoyed, but you agree to go, then joke that he's lucky Brad Pitt didn't call you first.

c. Irritated, you say you aren't free, and he should have called sooner.

d. You didn't wait. You called him on Wednesday and suggested a movie.

e. You tell him that you'd love to go out with him sometime, but the date wasn't definite so you made other plans.

Tardy Ty:
How do you set limits with lateness?

You arrive on time for a first date with Ty, but he shows up 30 minutes late.

a. You sympathize about the bad traffic.

b. You're irritated but don't say so. All evening you joke about how you hope he's worth waiting for.

c. You tell him you are upset. Although he apologizes, you're still mad.

d. You called him after 20 minutes to ask what's up.

e. You left after 20 minutes. You don't want him to think you'll be OK with chronic lateness.

Cheap Charlie:
Do you pay on a date?

Dinner was great. The check arrives and sits on the table. Charlie doesn't touch it.

  a. He clearly wants you to pay, so you split it.

  b. You offer to split the check even though you want him to pay.

  c. You offer to pay to avoid an awkward moment.

  d. Waiting for him to pay is so old-fashioned. You split it.

  e. You enjoy your conversation, letting the check sit there until he pays it, never offering. You want to give him a chance to impress you.

Flaky Frank:
How do you handle a "boomerang" boyfriend?

Your ex-boyfriend calls, saying he left his new girlfriend and he knows he made a mistake. He wants to get back together.

  a. You take him back, no questions asked.

  b. Even though you're mad at him, you take him back. You joke about how lucky he is to have you.

  c. You tell him you wouldn't date him if he were the last guy on Earth.

  d. You give him another chance. You have lengthy conversations about his commitment.

  e. Open to the possibility that he made a mistake, you start the dating process all over, taking your time to figure out if he's worth another risk with your heart.

Bold Brandon:
What do you do when he steps over the line?

You're in a cab with Brandon, a friend of a friend whom you just met, when suddenly he puts his hand on your thigh. Extremely uncomfortable, you stammer, "Uh, this is moving a little fast for me." He says, "What are you, a tease?"

    a. You realize you said the wrong thing. You apologize and let Brandon take the lead.

    b. You're speechless but don't stop him. Afterward, you call your mutual friends to complain about how aggressive he is.

    c. You say, "You're a real jerk!" You can't stand him and never want to see him again.

    d. You laugh it off. If you wrote off every guy who did something immature, you'd never go on a date.

    e. You stay calm but stick to your guns. You don't have to explain yourself. Instead, you give him the chance to apologize by asking him, "What's wrong with moving slowly?"

Proposing Pete:
What do you do when he won't propose?

You've dated Pete for two years. You want to get married, but Pete prefers things just as they are. Now you're tired of waiting. Will Pete ever propose?

    a. If you make him happy, he will eventually propose.

    b. You joke to Pete about his commitment issues and complain to your friends that he hasn't proposed.

    c. You chew him out, complaining he can't make a commitment.

d. You suggest moving in together to see if you are compatible for marriage.

e. You explain how important marriage is to you and that you are worried the relationship has no future if he isn't ready. You go out with your friends more often to get some distance and to get used to living without him, just in case.

Nonexclusive Eric:
How and when do you bring up monogamy?

Eric drives you home from a romantic fourth-date dinner and, after several minutes of passionate kissing at your door, he asks if he can come in. You haven't discussed exclusivity—a topic you'd like to cover before you decide whether to sleep with him.

a. It's been four dates—how many guys this great will wait that long? You invite him in and have sex.

b. You're afraid to bring it up. You invite him in, but you can't relax and act more distant for the rest of the evening.

c. You're head over heels! You go for it. The next morning you feel insecure and want to talk about the relationship.

d. You got more attached than you had expected last time you had casual sex, but you figure you can handle it this time. You invite him in and have sex.

e. You don't want another broken heart. Intimacy causes you to get emotionally attached, so you invite him in but make it clear that you aren't into casual sex.

Distant Darryl:
Do you drive to him or will it drive you nuts?

You drive to a party an hour away and meet a charming, funny local guy. You mention where you each live. He suggests a first date at his favorite restaurant, assuming you will drive back to meet him.

    a. You agree. You're disappointed he didn't make more of an effort, but you hope he'll drive to you next time.

    b. You agree, but you're not happy about it. Somehow you manage to get lost and you're 30 minutes late.

    c. You tell him that he'll have to drive to your town to get a date with you.

    d. You offer to meet halfway.

    e. You like guys to put in more effort, so you tell him that, although you'd love to go out with him, you'll have to pass.

Overextended Oscar:
Is he "two-timing" you if he tells you?

You are dating your coworker Oscar. Two months after your relationship became sexual, he tells you that his ex called him. He doesn't want to break up with you, but he does want to sleep with her every now and then "for old times' sake."

    a. You don't want to lose him, so you agree to the open relationship.

    b. You don't like it, but you agree. You show up late for dates, make sarcastic comments, and gripe about him to your friends.

c. You break up with him. You criticize and yell at him at the office.

d. You figure sex is just sex—you are the one he chose to be his girlfriend. It shouldn't bother you. You tell him it's fine.

e. You tell him you're not comfortable with it and stop seeing him. You don't want somebody who doesn't want exclusivity.

One-Night-Stand Otto:
How do you handle the "uh-oh" phenomenon?

You and Otto have flirted on and off for years. Then one night, one thing leads to another and you end up in bed, having a great time. The next morning, he can't get out of there fast enough.

a. You hope you didn't do anything to make him uncomfortable. You should have told him you knew it was just a one-night stand.

b. You are hurt and call your friends to complain about him.

c. He can't treat you this way! You insist that you need to have a talk.

d. You decide to try out the friends-with-benefits thing.

e. You don't want to start a relationship by waiting to see if he can overcome feeling awkward. You tell him that last night was a big mistake.

Now let's look at what the quiz tells you. Which letters did you choose most often? Let's see which flower descriptions fit you the best:

A. DAISY
You're eager to please. Denying your own needs seems to come naturally.

You may move too quickly in relationships and forget the importance of protecting your heart. Your desire to please a man can cause you to forget that slow can be sexy.

You may not realize that you always have a choice. Cultivate your intuition about what you want and where your boundaries are. If it's hard to get in touch with your feelings in the moment, considerer how you feel after you deny your needs.

Until you're sure how you feel, you might start by saying, "I'm not sure how I feel about that" (instead of saying "yes" or "no"). If you rapidly get involved with men, remember to protect your heart—that slow can be sexy. Your voice matters, so brainstorm ways to express yourself and stand up for yourself before a date. Practice with a friend or make a list of nonnegotiables beforehand. Be sure to also practice how you would stick to them. When you do stand up for yourself, move on if a guy doesn't respect your voice.

B. IRIS
Sometimes you have trouble expressing your feelings. Others think you're angry, but you don't recognize it.

People might say your jokes about them aren't so funny and hurt their feelings. Or your feelings may get expressed in other ways that people don't like, like being late or forgetting things.

Rather than suppressing your feelings, use your emotions to help you make the decisions that are best for you. You may have trouble recognizing how you feel in the moment and could benefit from revisiting the situation later to figure out how you feel. It might help you to discuss it with someone you trust. Consider the possibility that you're angry and too afraid to express it. Becoming more aware of your emotions will allow you to follow your intuition about what is right for you. Remember that your voice matters. The more aware of your feelings you become, the better you'll be able to communicate what you want in a way that serves you. Remember how effective "I" language can be: "I'm not comfortable," "I don't know," "I'm not sure."

C. POPPY
You are good at understanding your emotions, but sometimes you tend to overreact. Your emotions may make it hard for you to stand up for yourself in a calm, tactful way.

Perhaps your anger has made you sound more demanding than you'd like. Maybe you've gotten carried away and fallen for guys without any regard to protecting yourself emotionally. You may have gotten more clingy or needy than you wanted to. And you might be pushing men away with the rawness of your emotions.

Your voice matters, but overreacting is often not the ideal way to express yourself. Whenever you feel emotional, start by taking a breath. Don't react right away. Give yourself a moment to think about how you feel and why you feel that way. Then, if you are ready, focus on *how* you express yourself. If you don't think you can say what you want without regret, then tell the guy you need some time to collect yourself. Remember, words linger. You don't need to react in the moment. Later, see if you can understand what situations are triggering your emotions and if there are any patterns.

Practice communicating your feelings in a way that will allow your voice to be heard, like with "I" language ("I feel uncomfortable with…" "I'm not ready for…") rather than words that sound critical ("You are being rude…" "You are taking me for granted…"). That way, if a guy doesn't respect your voice, you can move on with the knowledge that he just wasn't right for you, rather than wondering if he reacted that way because you didn't express yourself effectively.

D. VIOLET
You're a firm believer in equality. You've accepted heartache as an inevitable part of the dating process, but sometimes this attitude can leave you in hurtful situations that you could have avoided.

Sometimes your view of being a strong and powerful woman might interfere with what's right for you emotionally. Remember that slow can be sexy. By taking your time with men, you will be able to avoid some of the bumps in the road and you will be better able to protect your heart. Media and peer pressure solutions might not be right for you, so try making decisions based on how you feel, not just what you think should be the right course of action. Be clear about your boundaries with men.

E. ROSE
You follow the five guidelines to being your own Brand of Sexy:

1. You always have a choice.

2. Media and peer pressure solutions might not be right for you.

3. Slow can be sexy.

4. Your voice matters.

5. If a guy isn't respecting your voice, move on.

You are clear about your desire to be treated respectfully and able to express your needs calmly. You're good at guarding your heart. You may not have a date every Friday night, but the men you date either treat you well or they disappear rather quickly. Your good instincts and intuition make the dating journey an exciting adventure. Keep listening to your instincts, and help other women develop their own Brands of Sexy.

Quiz Results Review

Was it difficult for you to answer these questions honestly? Were you embarrassed by some of the ways you currently handle these situations? Were you trying to figure out what the "right" answer was? Remember, the point of this quiz is to figure out what is right for you, not what's right for somebody else. Every woman's Brand of Sexy can look different. The growth mindset is all about realizing it's OK to have something to learn. It's OK to take this quiz as many times as you like. In fact, you might get more out of it the next few times you take it.

After trying these suggestions for a few months, if you're not able to make the changes you'd like, you might benefit from consulting a psychotherapist or psychiatrist. You might have a medical, psychiatric, or psychological condition that could be contributing to the difficulty you're having. There are good treatments to help you manage your reactions in a more constructive way. For more information about making this decision, go to www.beyourownbrandofsexy.com.

9

When Self-Help Books Aren't Enough

"Knowing others is intelligence;
knowing yourself is true wisdom.
Mastering others is strength,
mastering yourself is true power."
—Lao-Tzu

I n previous chapters we've discussed some not-so-simple steps that can help you develop your instincts and intuition about men, so that you can learn to be your own Brand of Sexy. For many of you, these tools and strategies can help you with your problems with dating. However, others may find this process more difficult. You might still be carrying emotional baggage from your past that has unknowingly created more deeply ingrained, unhealthy dating patterns. Are you looking for love in all the wrong places or sabotaging your relationships with men? Read on to see whether this applies to you and what you can do about it.

Have the suggestions in previous chapters felt difficult to implement? Maybe you've noticed that, in thinking about changing your patterns, you experience levels of fear, anger, or other emotions that seem out of proportion to the situation. Maybe you get mad thinking that I'm suggesting change is easy. Or perhaps some of my suggestions have felt impossible. Maybe you aren't sure what to change, but you have similar problems in each of your relationships with men. Do you wonder if it's your problem, his problem, or just incompatibility? This is a complex question that is important to answer—sometimes a relationship has problems because the two people in it are simply not a good match. And, of course, often both parties have a hand in creating relationship problems. However, if you find that you tend to struggle with the same types of issues in your relationships, over and over again, therapy may be able to help you figure out whether you choose incompatible men and how you might be able to make changes.

Please remember nobody escapes having *some* issues—it is part of the human experience—but some of us have tougher ones to deal with than the rest. How can you tell whether your reactions are "normal" or symptoms of a more troubling underlying issue? If they are interfering with your everyday functioning or repeatedly affecting your relationships, then some concern is warranted. It will require you to be honest with yourself to judge this, which can be hard. We don't like admitting we have problems because we don't want to see ourselves as weak or helpless. Worse, negative attitudes toward people with problems make it harder to see when we need help, or to get psychotherapy or other counseling even when we see we need it. Psychiatrists refer to these negative attitudes as "stigma." Why is this a problem for you? If you aren't open to seeing that you might need help, you might avoid treatments that could help you get the relationship or happiness you want. It's difficult to be objective about ourselves. Over 20 million adults in the United States have anxiety, depression, bipolar disorder, or schizophrenia.[167] Even the most benign and easy to treat are stigmatized, leading to shame. And many of us without a diagnosed disorder may still have symptoms that a therapist can help with. It's hard to confront our flaws or weaknesses but, until we do, how can we change them?

Some of us feel better when we receive a diagnosis from a doctor. Having a name for what ails you sometimes brings comfort—somebody knows what this is and what to do about it. But many feel labeled by a diagnosis. They feel criticized and may react with anger, shame, or self-blame.

We physicians are sometimes too clinical in our language. Let's leave diagnoses out of our discussion and talk about feelings. Professional guidance and support can help you heal serious issues, but it can also help you to make changes that you are struggling to make on your own and to better understand your decisions, needs, and emotions. When baggage from the past is involved or if you're not as calm or confident as you used to be, relationships become much more complicated. Sometimes these situations can feel as though we're trapped in a foreign land with no idea how we got there. Resolving them doesn't feel quite so simple as buying a return ticket to get back. But there are treatments that can help you. The first step is recognizing you need some help.

Maybe some of you will be able to see yourselves in these stories. You may see yourself in more than one story. They aren't intended for you to jump to any conclusions regarding diagnosis or treatment, only to help you become curious about yourself and why you do what you do. You might consider whether you have patterns that aren't working that you'd like to change (like choosing men who aren't right for you or sabotaging the progress of your relationships) and whether psychotherapy might be valuable in that process. Remember, we all have trouble seeing ourselves objectively. Sometimes it takes a friend or a therapist to give us a new perspective on our lives.

Obsessionland

> When things get serious with her boyfriend, Lena soon lands in Obsessionland. She texts him twice a day, even though she tries hard not to. If she doesn't hear back right away, she's frantic and fears the relationship is over. When he does surface, she acts angry and demands to know why he didn't respond sooner, even though she recognizes that she might be overreacting. He becomes defensive and starts to distance himself. Lena realizes that her actions are a problem, but she is so determined to be his Ms. Right that she doesn't see she's pushing him away. She can't seem to help herself.

Our other resident of Obsessionland is the opposite of Lena—she doesn't believe in calling or texting men.

> Sandy is driving her friends crazy with her play-by-play account of what happened with her boyfriend Kurt. She is always asking them, "Why hasn't he called?" or "Do you think he cares about me?" She has such a one-track mind that she has trouble focusing at work. Her friends are screening her calls because all she can talk about is her relationship. One of her closest friends suggests therapy, but Sandy doesn't think she needs it.

Lena and Sandy are so preoccupied that their obsessiveness hurts their relationships. And you can live in Obsessionland without being obsessed with a man. Having an overly consuming focus on any one thing in your life can interfere with your ability to develop and maintain healthy relationships. Your focus might be a man, but it might also be your job, shopping, or anything else that seems to dominate your time, energy, and daily life. Maybe you're obsessed with the idea that you must find a husband right away, making you desperate and vulnerable to a bad marriage. If you have a singular focus that causes you to neglect other important areas of your life, you may be residing in Obsessionland.

Remember, it's not just women who have these problems. Dating men who live in Obsessionland can also be a problem. If you notice that your partner has a consuming focus that seems to negatively affect your relationship—this may be anything from work to going out to bars with friends—it could be a red flag that he either needs to make some changes or that he is not the right person for you. If you notice that you continually choose men who live in Obsessionland and you can't figure out why, you might benefit from exploring these choices with a therapist.

Shame City

We all play the hand we're dealt, right? Some of us have had poor examples of relationships modeled by our parents, some of us have suffered something traumatic which prevents us from having healthy relationships, and some of us walk around with open wounds from the blows that life has given us. Is shame part of your surroundings?

Amaya's friends are worried about her. They see her in one dysfunctional relationship after another. She is attracted to men who are highly successful and powerful but tends to pick bullies who end up dominating her, and she feels highly vulnerable. The guy always leaves her for another woman.

Amaya resists her friends' suggestion to see a therapist. She tells them she thinks therapy is bogus, but deep down she is scared to death. She finds the idea of opening herself up to someone extremely threatening.

Finally, her friends convince her that her destructive relationship pattern might benefit from talking out her issues with a trained therapist. "OK," she thinks, "I'll work on it, but nobody is going to make me tell my secret."

Amaya's secret is something that happened years ago and she has never told a soul. She has nightmares about it but feels so much shame that she's kept quiet all these years.

Her therapist is patient with Amaya's reluctance, drawing her out and establishing trust between them. They talk about how her past might be contributing to her poor choices in men. Eventually, she reveals to the therapist that she had been molested as a child. As she works through this, Amaya is able to heal and feel accepted. She learns that she had been unable to stand up to these men because she felt helpless, the way she did with her abuser. Teasing out her past through therapy helps put her on a path toward a healthier relationship.

Is there something in your past you'd rather forget that might be getting in your way? Secrets come in many forms. Some may feel shame about a rape, a teenage pregnancy, an abortion, an inappropriate relationship—any number of things. These things are not easy to talk about. Telling someone can be very healing, but it is critical to choose the right person. Timing is important and feeling safe is imperative.

We all have our secrets but, when we feel deeply ashamed of ours, we can develop a fear of getting close to others. If they really knew us, warts and all, would they still care? How can you feel you deserve to get what you want if you are filled with shame?

Is there something in your past that haunts you? If one of your friends told you that she experienced the same thing, would you be as harsh on her as you are on yourself?

Loss Planet

Sometimes we experience a loss—death or divorce of parents, a painful breakup, a critical or emotionally cold family—that leaves us feeling isolated or alone and can affect our relationships. Believe it or not, loss may come in the form of someone close to us who is overly judgmental or who does not provide the support we need and expect. Is there someone important in your life who dismisses your needs or just doesn't recognize them? You may be living on Loss Planet.

Joelle wanted a long-term relationship with a caring, sensitive guy. She'd been seeing Lucas for a while—he was successful and attractive, but lately she'd noticed he was distracted and moody when they got together. She knew he had a high-pressure job, like other guys she'd dated, and she knew the last thing a stressed-out guy needed was a critical girlfriend, so she swallowed her frustration and wondered why she kept ending up with emotionally unavailable men. Her friends were concerned that she was unwilling to talk to Lucas about the situation and encouraged her to see a therapist about her pattern. Joelle found therapy to be helpful. During her sessions, Joelle talked about her mother, who could be sweet at times but was often extremely critical. Her mother was in her own world and was oblivious to Joelle's needs, and her father never stood up for her. Joelle often felt alone, as if no one really knew her or cared about her. In effect, she was emotionally abandoned—her mother just didn't get her. In time, through therapy, Joelle realized how her relationship with her mother had affected her romantic life. Exploring her feelings of being alone and unprotected by her parents made it easier to understand why she was afraid to rock the boat with Lucas.

If you have experienced many losses or people not being emotionally supportive, and you have trouble standing up for what you want in a relationship, you might benefit from treatment to address these obstacles.

When Self-Help Books Aren't Enough for You

Sometimes we are the last to know we need help. It's often hard to recognize in ourselves what is so obvious to others. Below are some warning signs that you might need professional help. Do you recognize yourself here?

- Are you convinced that, given enough time, you can change your boyfriend into Mr. Right?

- Do you always put his feelings first and ignore your own?

- Are you attracted only to men who are unavailable (married, commitment-phobic, gay)?

- Do you have a pattern of relationships with boyfriends who fail to understand your needs and support you emotionally?

- Do you promise yourself to stop hooking up but wake up Sunday morning with a new guy?

- Do you have a pattern of letting people take advantage of your good nature? Are you a doormat?

- Does every man you date fail to live up to the perfection of your ex?

- Are people often telling you you're overly emotional?

- Do you stay in bad relationships to avoid being alone?

- Do you tend to date guys who don't treat you well?

- Do you often neglect your own needs because you're too busy taking care of everyone else?

- Do you tend to be afraid to ask for what you want in a relationship because you fear the other person will be angry?

- Do you continually find ways to mess up your relationships with men, and then wonder why you behaved that way?

- Do all your past relationships with men seem to have similar problems?

Are you ready to move away from Obsessionland, Loss Planet, or Shame City? Don't forget that, because our culture is so focused on the exterior (beauty and money), we often don't recognize when attention to our inner lives is a much better solution to this kind of entrapment. Self-help books often aren't enough if you're struggling with more serious issues. For tips on how to find the right therapist and information about mental health issues and psychotherapy, visit my website: www.beyourownbrandofsexy.com.

10

Your Next Chapter

"Life is like a soap opera.
You're writing the next chapter.
Make it a positive one."
—Terry Paulson, PhD

Congratulations! You made it to the last chapter. And hopefully you've learned more about yourself, what works for you, and how to stand up for yourself. Let's take a quick look at what we've covered so far, and then we can start taking the next steps.

How Far We've Come

As we saw, the women's movement and the sexual revolution helped women make tremendous strides towards equality and opportunity, breaking free of rigid gender roles. But, with so much change happening so quickly, and with the increased sexualization of our culture, we didn't anticipate some of the problems we'd face.

We were so delighted with our new freedom that we let the pendulum swing too far in the opposite direction. We went from "women are the weaker sex" to "there's no difference between men and women"; from "if you call him first, you're desperate" to "if you don't call first, you're passive and powerless"; from "if you have sex before marriage, you're a tramp" to "if you're a virgin, you're a prude." We simply traded one set of unrealistic standards for another. In the process, we forgot the meaning of liberation: the freedom to choose for yourself.

And now you have a better picture of who the "modern woman" is—she's not a "gold standard" for us to emulate but a false belief that we use as a guide when we're in doubt. The "modern woman" (who can ask men out, who can have casual sex, and who doesn't expect to be pursued or courted) is a role model that won't work for every woman. The fact that so many of us compare ourselves to her and believe her lifestyle is ideal illustrates our need for a new revolution.

Being different from men is a good thing—we don't have to demonize femininity just because some people associate it with being weak or passive. Redefining femininity means we can each be feminine and powerful in different ways, with our own unique approaches. Instead of thinking power simply comes from being sexually uninhibited, we've seen that real power means making the best decisions for ourselves based on our individual needs and what works for us.

Hopefully by now you've gotten a better sense of what you want in dating and relationships and how to get it.

So what's next?

Take the First Step

Darla is 11 months old and eager to learn how to walk. The first time she uses the couch to pull herself up to stand, her mother applauds and kisses her. Her parents delight in these efforts, encouraging her when she falls and comforting her when she cries. Every bit of progress is recorded for posterity, and Darla's new skills are posted on Facebook for all the world to see.

Babies are given all sorts of encouragement as they are learning new things. Can you imagine a parent telling a baby taking her first steps, "You're not moving fast enough! Straighten your legs!"? Of course not. Doting parents offer help, not criticism.

We need support too when we start learning anything new. Many of us feel we have to change instantly to keep up with quickly changing times, and we can be awfully hard on ourselves when we stumble or revert to old habits. If we remember that we are taking a "baby step"—a tiny bit of progress at a time—and that "baby steps" deserve support and applause, we will learn to be patient with ourselves and celebrate our little victories along the way.

Believe it or not, a series of small changes can often lead to bigger changes in our lives. You might think it's no big deal if you start standing up for yourself in seemingly small ways, like returning a purchase you've changed your mind about or expressing a differing opinion from someone. However, practice with the small stuff can make you more comfortable with saying "no" in bigger ways, like turning down dates or standing your ground when someone does something you aren't comfortable with ("I don't like this," "I don't agree"). This begins the process of weeding out the guys who are going nowhere in your life. And that can guide you to appreciating nice guys. What happens next all depends on you and what you want!

Taking the first steps might eventually help all women. The more comfortable we become in standing up for ourselves, the more likely we'll be treated well. The more of us who are treated well, the better our culture becomes for all women. This is a way for women to gain more power—not simply in relationships with men but also at work, with our families, and in the world. Imagine more women using their power to solve some of the world's problems.

Maybe you think "baby steps" won't get you anywhere, but Malcolm Gladwell in *The Tipping Point: How Little Things Can Make a Big Difference* tells us otherwise.[168] He argues that even the smallest changes can lead to big effects, and sometimes these changes occur rapidly, in one dramatic moment—the "Tipping Point." These "Tipping Points" cause societal transformations, such as fashion trends and crime waves, which then spread like virus epidemics (think viral video). One example of this phenomenon is Hush Puppies shoes, which made a dramatic comeback in the mid-'90s. In one year, the shoes went from annual sales of 30,000 pairs to being on the feet of kids across America and annual sales of 430,000. By the next year, sales had quadrupled.

While we believe changes happen gradually or that's "just the way it is," as if we have no effect, we can actually create this kind of societal contagion "by tinkering with the smallest details of the immediate environment."[169] We don't have to drastically change who we are. We just need to start being more aware. Gladwell demonstrates his theory again with the example of criminologists Wilson and Kelling's brilliant theory of crime called "Broken Windows." According to this theory, when people see broken windows or graffiti, they assume nobody cares and anything goes, inviting more serious crime. So, in the '90s, New York cracked down on minor infractions that had previously been ignored. The city cleaned up graffiti and police went after people who didn't pay to ride the subway. It turned out that one out of seven of those arrested for these minor infractions had an outstanding warrant, and one out of 20 were carrying a concealed weapon. As a result of these efforts, the crime rate quickly and dramatically decreased. "Minor, seemingly insignificant quality-of-life crimes, they said, were Tipping Points for violent crime."[170]

Of course, we're not talking about criminal behavior here, but think about the similarities. We ignore or laugh off seemingly minor sexual remarks or touches, even when we're not comfortable with them. If we could find nice ways to make it clear when we're not OK with the smaller issues, would we be helping to stop bigger sexual transgressions?

We don't know when the idea that we need a new sexual revolution will "tip," rapidly changing the world. As pioneers, we must be careful not to push ourselves too far out of our comfort zones—you have to live with the consequences. It's best to be our own Brand of Sexy rather than to live to try to prove a point. You can choose your contribution based on what's right for you. You can help by spreading the word in many ways. I urge you to do only what you're comfortable with, or to do things that are only a "baby step" away—why risk falling with too big a step? The goal of this book is to open your eyes and ask you to take small steps, maybe toward something bigger, not to give you reasons to feel bad about yourself by having unrealistic expectations. Let's try not to be perfectionists because, even if it's not perfect, we're still making changes. What's the easiest way for you to take a stand? Start there.

Communication Is Everything

Believe it or not, some men might not realize they're making you uncomfortable. With so many women expecting themselves to be sexually uninhibited and others avoiding social situations where they have to face overt sexual advances, maybe some men simply don't know any better. Then the question becomes: Do they care how you feel? A nice guy will apologize, even if you don't say it perfectly. A guy who's not so nice might give you a halfhearted "sorry," look at you funny, or call you a prude or frigid if you're not comfortable. If you can't stand up for yourself because you're more afraid of getting your feelings hurt, it's going to take you longer to see what kind of guy he is.

It can be challenging to communicate clearly and pleasantly when you're nervous, angry, or just surprised. Let's revisit Julie and Ian for some tips on how to get your message across:

> Julie is at a salsa club dancing with Ian, who's a friend of the friends she came with and seems like a nice guy. She's thinking what a great dancer he is when suddenly Ian runs his hands up her legs to her hips, which makes her extremely uncomfortable. Trying to be diplomatic, Julie says with a smile, "Uh, what's with the hands?" Ian teasingly says, "What are you, a virgin?" She says, "What does that have to do with it?" and he apologizes.

Communication experts tell us that using "I" language helps tremendously to get your point across.[171] For example, if Julie had said, "I'm enjoying dancing with you, but I'm not comfortable with all the touching," Ian might have apologized sooner, without making the "virgin" remark. Why? When we start with "I feel" (or in this case, "I don't feel…"), it's clear that we're not criticizing, judging, or implying right or wrong, we're just saying how we feel. But "What's with the hands?" could sound like, "Get your sex-maniac hands off me!" or "What do you think you're doing with those hands?" so, even if you're smiling, it sounds more critical and challenging. Isn't it easier to listen when you don't feel like you're under attack?

Of course, we all know how difficult it can be to stand up for ourselves when we're very angry—anger can cloud our judgment, make us sound accusatory, and cause us to say things we don't mean. So, for example, calling a man who says something inappropriate a "male chauvinist pig" may feel like standing up for yourself, but in reality he will probably only react to your anger and the insult rather than understand why his comment was wrong. Expressing ourselves constructively can be challenging when anger is one of the emotions we're feeling, but it's important if we want to be heard. This skill can be helpful in any relationship, and practice helps tremendously. Besides, if we can dial it down, we're more likely to get what we want. As the old saying goes, "You catch more flies with honey than with vinegar."

If we start by saying, "I'm having fun," we're letting him know the big picture is positive other than this one minor problem. So the guy is less likely to become defensive and more likely to hear what we're saying. Research shows that when discussing conflict, happily married couples made five positive remarks for every one negative remark, while those headed for divorce made the same number of positive and negative remarks.[172] Just because you're single doesn't mean this research won't help you too.

While some women object to the approach of revealing their emotions and making "I feel" statements as too "feminine," communication experts recommend this technique for men too.[173] Besides, what's wrong with being feminine? It's not passive to attempt to get what you want—to be heard, for your feelings to be acknowledged, or to get an apology.

Next Steps

If you're struggling a bit with taking these first steps, don't worry—there's no shame in asking for help and getting some support. We're socialized to be people-pleasers and, when we stand up for ourselves, there is a real possibility that the other person won't be pleased—no wonder it's a little scary. Let's look at a few tips on making it easier to express what you need.

Figure Out What Works for You

Just like there's not one way to be your own Brand of Sexy, there isn't a one-size-fits-all style of communication. Let's go back to Julie and Ian's story—what if you're not comfortable even saying you're not comfortable? You can try something softer like, "I'm not sure how I feel about that."

Here are some ways to help you understand yourself and define your own Brand of Sexy:

Listen to yourself

- Are you being honest with yourself about what you want, what you feel, and whether what you're doing is working?

- When you speak up, do you sound angry? Wishy-washy? Defensive? Critical?

- Do you find yourself making excuses for men and telling yourself that your feelings aren't important?

Maria's boyfriend Xavier is always hugging and kissing her in public. She loves the attention and welcomes it in private but is uncomfortable with Xavier grabbing her in public. For a while she ignores her discomfort, but then one day her feelings boil over and she gets annoyed with Xavier, telling him to cool it. Xavier feels rejected by the comment, so Maria tells herself that he is just an affectionate guy, and she is being too uptight. Eventually, her best friend encourages her to bring up the conversation with Xavier again but this time in a way that explains her feelings without sounding so annoyed or critical. She finally gets through when she tells him, "What we have is so special, I'd like to keep it just between the two of us, OK?"

Listen to your supporters

- Do your friends notice patterns in your choices or behaviors with men?

- If men aren't asking you for a second date, is there anything you can learn that will help you next time?

- Would it help to have someone hold you accountable? A close friend, or a therapist?

Kim had noticed her tendency to drive off potential boyfriends by talking about her ex on the first date. Her friend Nahid offered to help her break the habit. They came up with a system. Nahid would help Kim prepare questions ahead of time: What sports teams did he follow? What was the best job he ever had? Was he close to his family? The pre-date prep reminded Kim to focus on her date and keep her thoughts about her ex to herself. The next morning, Nahid would call Kim and see if she could answer the questions. Kim found that reporting back to Nahid broke her of her bad habit.

Don't listen to your critics

- Talk back to the voice inside you (the one that sounds suspiciously like your mother) that tells you to "Hurry up and marry somebody! Anybody!"

- Learn to recite positive mantras ("I am making progress every day") if you are prone to self-criticism or need encouragement.

- Steer clear of people who bring you down— you need to stay strong and positive.

Tanya is at a baby shower for her friend Nicole, who is glowing with happiness and fulfillment. In her eagerness to share her excitement, Nicole turns to Tanya and says, "Girl, your eggs are going to be dried up before you find a man! Let's find you somebody!" Tanya laughs and responds,

"My eggs are just fine, thank you, and besides, babies might not be in the cards for everyone, Nicole. I'll find the right man when I am ready." She silently repeats her mantra: "I have my own path."

Reward yourself

- When you make progress, celebrate!

- Don't minimize the importance of accomplishments that may seem minor to you.

- Be your own cheerleader and encourage others to do the same.

Try It Out

As previously mentioned, expressing ourselves constructively can be challenging when anger, fear, excitement, or other emotions interfere, but it's an important skill to learn if we want to be heard in any relationship. Just like any other new skill, the more you practice, the better you'll get. So try it out in easier situations (letting the waiter know you had asked for dressing on the side, or politely telling your mother's friend again that no thanks, you don't want to be fixed up with her good-looking but arrogant nephew, even though he's "quite a catch").

Reward Yourself Again

Believe it or not, you can't really congratulate yourself too much in this process. You deserve to be rewarded for your hard work, and it will help you stay enthusiastic and motivated in making these difficult changes.

Now that you have some strategies to try, let's talk about some guidelines. Remember, we threw out the old rules in our quest for liberation. Now what do we do?

A New Sexual Revolution

We have an opportunity to change what is not working for us, both individually and culturally. By joining together, we can improve our love lives, develop healthier relationships, and take a stand against cultural expectations and pressures that are not serving us. We don't have to accept the status quo. It's time for a new sexual revolution that encourages each woman to be her own Brand of Sexy and to embrace sisterhood.

Five Guidelines to Being Your Own Brand of Sexy

1. You Always Have a Choice.

At this point in history, we are pioneers with a choice—we can accept the status quo, saying that's "just the way it is," or we can decide how we want our next chapter to unfold. But the key to the new sexual revolution is to remember that "one size doesn't fit all." That applies not only to our sex lives but to how we change what isn't working for us. Your friend might want to join a women's group that meets regularly, and you might want to discuss how the new sexual revolution could work for you with only your closest friends.

2. Media and Peer Pressure Solutions Might Not Be Right for You.

We've discussed at length the importance of recognizing how we're influenced by our culture, friends, and family. By recognizing cultural expectations, we can begin to understand how these pressures are affecting our lives. This understanding gives us the power to make our own choices when there is a discrepancy between what our culture encourages and what is best for us. Even the most well-intentioned advice from friends or family may not be what's right for us, which is why it is so important to encourage each other's intuition and instincts.

Some of us might even want to consider a bigger picture. Do we have any responsibility to consider how our decisions about sexuality affect others? Should we attempt to protect future generations of women or is that infantilizing them? What will happen to them if we don't? Could anyone 50 years ago have predicted teenagers hooking up and "sexting"? Today's girls are maturing even faster than we did, thanks to environmental changes,[174] so it's even more important to wrestle with these decisions now—do we want sex to be divorced from intimacy? There's a fine line between permission, persuasion, and pressure in a culture that is saturated with sex when we all strive to be normal. How can we encourage girls to do what works for them without stigmatizing them for their choices?

3. Slow Can Be Sexy.

We need to expand our concept of "protection" to include the need to guard ourselves emotionally. In order to protect ourselves we must know ourselves, figure out what works for us, and decide where to draw the line, taking into account our own personalities and feelings. These days, there isn't much stigma to premarital sex, to living together without marriage, or even to casually hooking up. Those behaviors might work for some people but not necessarily for others. Doing what your best friend does might be completely wrong for you. Deciding where your line is, refusing to cross it, and taking your time emotionally will serve to protect your heart.

4. Your Voice Matters.

Each of us needs to cultivate our own intuition to help us figure out what situations and what people are good for us and which ones aren't worth our time. When we trust our intuition, we gain the confidence to say "no" to situations outside our comfort zone, to ask for what we need, and to voice our thoughts and feelings. The Single Woman's 12-Piece Dating Toolbox can help you learn what's best for you and develop your intuition, which can help you to stand up for yourself. And it will give you strategies to achieve the kind of relationship you are looking for. If you haven't figured out what works for you yet, don't give up on it. This process can take time.

5. If a Guy Isn't Respecting Your Voice, Move On.

If a guy doesn't treat you how you deserve to be treated, or if he doesn't respect your needs even after you have stood up for yourself, he's not worth your time. There are all different types of men out there—those who only want casual sex, those who want committed and loving relationships, and everything in between. The trick is to find the ones who want the same thing as you. Spending time on a man who wants something different than you or on a man who isn't willing to respect you only causes pain and frustration, and it detracts from the time you could be spending with a more compatible match. If he doesn't treat you with respect, move on to one who does.

Sisterhood Is Powerful

Being your own Brand of Sexy can feel challenging when it conflicts with the cultural norms, and it can feel even more intimidating if you don't have the support of the women around you. That's why we also need sisterhood. It is crucial to support each other throughout the process, respect each other's Brands of Sexy, and stand together against detrimental cultural expectations. Gloria Steinem defines a feminist as "anyone who recognizes the equality and full humanity of women and men"[175] and calls for all women, regardless of politics, religion, race, or economic status to join together in a "sisterhood." "Any woman who chooses to behave like a full human being," says Steinem, "should be warned that the armies of the status quo will treat her as something of a dirty joke. Ridicule is their natural and first weapon, with more serious opposition to follow. She will *need* sisterhood."[176]

In the past, we've accomplished a great deal. Because women banded together, laws have changed, society has progressed, and women are equal (mostly) before the law. Now that we have increased our power through sisterhood, we have the opportunity to use our influence to support individual women in creating healthier, more enjoyable love lives. Choices about sexuality are as unique as our DNA and, as long as we're not hurting ourselves or others, we deserve the support of our sisters. This is the next frontier of the feminist movement.

You Say You Want a Revolution

The Dalai Lama said, "The world will be saved by the Western Woman."[177] Women are known to have more sensitivity for others' pain and suffering.[178] We're naturals when it comes to empathy. We have the resources and compassion necessary to make a positive difference in the world.

If women are more sensitive to others, why aren't we nicer to each other? In Chapter 2, we talked about an important phenomenon: Women are calling the beautiful actress Christina Hendricks "fat," simply because she's not a size 0 or size 2 like the rest of the women in Hollywood. Women are pressuring her to conform to unrealistic standards and saying she could be a better sex object than she already is. Social psychologists blame competition for men for this tendency to put other women down.[179] What happened to sisterhood? Imagine if women would support each other in doing what's right for each of us as individuals rather than badgering us to conform. If only we could be more aware of what we're doing, wouldn't the value of sticking together outweigh the need for competition? We're all in this together, facing the same problems. What unites us is much larger than our differences.

During the 1960s, women faced a similar shift in perspective. They explored the nuances of all the changes around them by coming together in groups. As Gloria Steinem said in 1969, "I realize that, unless women organize, support each other, and force change, nothing basic is going to happen. Not even with the best of men. And I wonder: *'Are women—including me—willing to face that?'"*[180] These groups were referred to as "consciousness raising" because it was hard to grasp the concepts and how they affected your life without different perspectives.[181] Bonds formed when women understood their feelings about their shared experiences and wanted change. They needed support and permission from their peers to stand up for themselves, plus confidentiality and commitment to each other. Groups can be a healing force that often drastically changes perspectives—look at the effectiveness of 12-step programs and support groups for everything from alcohol abuse and eating disorders to breast cancer survival.[182]

None of us has all the answers. Our differences often give us a blind spot, making it difficult for us to see that what works for us might not be right for someone else. With heated, controversial subjects, we often tune others out or raise our voices when somebody disagrees with us. For example, if men and women are equal, does it really mean there are no differences between us? Is abstinence best for some women?

A dialogue about these issues will make it easier for us all to see that the solutions are far from simple. What does it mean to be sexy? Have we gone too far in our focus on sex? Is sex education enough? When problems are complicated, everyone has something to teach us about how to solve them. Why? Because the more we understand the problems from different perspectives, the more likely we can create effective solutions.

We've also seen how profoundly our sexualized culture affects young people, and here's a subject where being polarized makes things worse. How can we find common ground, while honoring individual opinions, to arrive at workable solutions?

A New Appreciation for Our Differences

A new sexual revolution is the understanding that we are different from one another, and we are beautiful in our differences. Let's take what we learned from the last sexual revolution and move forward. Arguing that "my way is the right way" for all women (you are a "prude" for remaining a virgin vs. you are "promiscuous" for having sex before marriage) perpetuates the confusion and shame for many girls and women. Creating more stigma is simply recreating the past in another form. While we still have progress to make in order to end sexism and achieve equality, the women's movement diminished many of the beliefs that previously held women back— that we are inferior and less capable. This opened up a much wider range of culturally acceptable choices for women. Why would we want to take a step backward by creating new judgmental attitudes about women to replace the old ones? We all benefit from cooperation.

Women can gain power as individuals and in groups. Working on yourself as an individual, with your own special strengths and issues, is critical to feeling empowered, no matter what gains we can make as a group. The first step toward changing the world is often changing yourself. Can we all agree that we want respect in dating situations and in life? Are we willing to give respect to others?

By the way, it's OK not to have all the answers to these questions. We're all still trying to figure out what it means to be a modern woman.

Sisterhood requires that we respect each other's positions. With this perspective, we can defuse conflict. For example, the next time you're in a situation where people have diametrically opposed opinions, instead of a heated defense of your position, try a new approach.

- "I think we're both worried about how overt sexuality in our society affects the young. Could there be more than one approach to solving the problem?"

- "It sounds like we're both concerned with what's best for children. Is there a way to combine a recommendation of abstinence with some other information about sexuality?"

- "Waiting for the guy to call might feel like 'playing hard to get' to you, but to me it feels like I'm protecting myself emotionally."

Is It OK to Look Sexy?

Well, of course it is! Sexual attraction is what propagates our species, and it's never going out of style. But you don't have to be attractive to anyone else in order to feel sexy.

Everyone wants to look attractive. But, as we've discussed, the beautiful women on magazine covers aren't real. The images are the product of dozens of people working to present an idealized version of beauty. Real women don't look like that.

The trouble is that we have come to believe that this is a standard to aim for. We're letting the beauty industry control how we see ourselves. We believe that if we buy their products we will look like the models in the ads. Remember, even the models don't look like the ads! Instead of striving for these impossible standards, try to find the beauty in your own uniqueness. Focus on your positive qualities. Whether you are kind, generous, or a good listener, we all have reasons to feel good about ourselves. And, if you have trouble seeing them, ask a friend what they like about you. Find out what activities or people help you feel good about yourself. Let's redefine "beautiful" and "sexy" to be reflections of who you are on the inside.

Looking Good and Doing Good

Nobody's saying you shouldn't care about your appearance. The point is that we spend so much time (and money) thinking about how we look and tweaking our sex appeal that we lose sight of what's most important. The Dalai Lama said that Western Women can change the world. But is this how we want to do it—by focusing mostly on our appearance? Can we find time in our lives to help someone else? Appreciating and celebrating our differences can unify us rather than separate us, and when women stand together we can make positive changes. Maybe we won't solve world hunger in the time we used to spend on exfoliating, but each of us has something to offer.

If you think this is preaching, consider this: For most women, filling your life with interesting, fulfilling, and rewarding activities is much more likely to lead you to happiness than striving to look like an airbrushed model on the cover of a magazine. And don't forget—happiness is often the sexiest quality of all. How happy can you be if your focus is on how poorly you compare to cover girls? And the added bonus to this philosophy? You are more likely to meet a nice guy while pursing outside interests than if your main focus is on improving your appearance.

Confidence Is Sexy—Self-Knowledge Is Power

"How do I become more confident?" many women ask. Although we've already discussed these ideas, you might not realize how they can improve your confidence.

Confidence is built by taking on challenges, even small ones. The more we encourage ourselves ("That was scary, but I did it and it went OK. Maybe next time it will be easier and I'll be able to communicate more clearly") rather than criticize ourselves ("That was lame and it wasn't even a hard thing to do"), the faster our confidence can grow.

Other factors that might improve your confidence are sharing with the right friend, group, or therapist. When you have any doubts about whether you deserve to feel hurt or angry about a man's behavior, hearing someone acknowledge it's OK to feel that way often clears away the doubts. Of course, we can't rely on others to figure out what's right for us, but the right understanding and support can make it easier.

Moving Forward

Congratulations on finishing this book! I've given you a lot to think about with the hope that we can begin an ongoing dialogue about these concerns. I think we will find that, rather than isolated problems, these issues are common conditions faced by many women. And just like we did in the '60s, we can band together to help make positive changes that benefit us all. I've given you a number of great tools to help you get what you want, and encouraged you to get help when you need it and move forward at your own pace. My website, www.beyourownbrandofsexy.com, offers more information as well as questions for discussion groups.

Emma was uncomfortable with modern dating in college but, instead of accepting the cultural norm, she took a stand based upon what she felt was right for her. She wasn't interested in casual sex, so she said "no" to "hanging out" with guys. She found her voice and learned to be firm about her boundaries. She found her own Brand of Sexy.

Deciding to buck the trend changed her life in more ways than one. She gained valuable self-knowledge about what she wanted and needed, honed her instincts in judging situations, and learned to listen to her intuition when she felt that something was not right for her. By taking a stand, she gained the confidence to do what was best for her in many other situations in her life. She is a successful grown woman now and in a serious, loving relationship.

Maybe I couldn't change the world for her when she needed it, but I could support her perspective that the world needed to change. Even more importantly, I encouraged her to be her own Brand of Sexy regardless of what her peers expected. She felt supported to do what was best for her and to say "no" to a situation that wasn't comfortable for her. I'm grateful that I could be there to support Emma and my patients. Sadly, many women today feel all alone with their concerns about modern dating. They say, "That's just the way it is," and then find some way to make the best of it. I wrote this book for them: women who will never be in my practice and women I'll never meet. I hope this book will support them to trust their gut, to be honest with themselves, and to stand up for what they want. Let's embrace this opportunity to support our sisters and change the world rather than simply accept a situation that doesn't work for so many of us.

Each of us can enjoy a healthy, fun love life if we learn what works for us regardless of what other people may think. The better we get at standing up for ourselves, the better our culture will be for all women. We have the opportunity to gain more power—in relationships with men, at work, with our families, and in the world. It may work for some women to take on more "masculine" traits, but it will never work for everyone. We have the chance to redefine what it means to be sexy, feminine, powerful women.

As Erica Jong said, "Different though we are, men and women were designed to be allies…We have often botched attempts to do this, but there is valor in trying to get it right, to heal the world and the rift between the sexes, to pursue the healing of home and by extension the healing of the earth."[183]

Sex doesn't equal power. Knowledge is power. Self-worth is power. Being your own Brand of Sexy is power. Women (and men) have changed the world many times before. We can do it again.

References

1

1. Robert B. Cialdini, *Influence: The Psychology of Persuasion* (New York, NY: HarperBusiness, 2006).

2. "Demand for Plastic Surgery Rebounds by Almost 9%," American Society for Aesthetic Plastic Surgery, April 4, 2011, http://www.surgery.org/media/news-releases/demand-for-plastic-surgery-rebounds-by-almost-9percent.

3. Caitlin Moran, *How to Be a Woman* (New York, NY: Harper Perennial, 2012).

4. Will Lassek, "Do Men Find Very Skinny Women Attractive?" *Psychology Today*, February 25, 2012, http://www.psychologytoday.com/blog/why-women-need-fat/201202/do-men-find-very-skinny-women-attractive.

5. Mark Regnerus, "Sex Is Cheap: Why young men have the upper hand in bed, even when they're failing in life," *Slate*, February 25, 2011, http://www.slate.com/articles/double_x/doublex/2011/02/sex_is_cheap.html.

6. Marcus Berzofsky et al., "Female Victims of Sexual Violence, 1994-2010," *Bureau of Justice Statistics*, March 7, 2013, http://www.bjs.gov/index.cfm?ty=pbdetail&iid=4594.

7. "Sexual Harassment Charges EEOC & FEPAs Combined: FY 1997-FY 2011," U.S. Equal Employment Opportunity Commission, http://www.eeoc.gov/eeoc/statistics/enforcement/sexual_harassment.cfm.

2

8. Deborah L. Tolman, letter to the editor, *The New York Times*, February 5, 2009, http://www.nytimes.com/2009/02/08/magazine/08Letters-t-WHATDOWOMENW_LETTERS.html.

9. Maureen Dowd, "What's a Modern Girl to Do?" *The New York Times*, October 30, 2005, http://www.nytimes.com/2005/10/30/magazine/30feminism.html.

10. Stanley Milgram, Leonard Bickman, and Lawrence Berkowitz, "Note on the Drawing Power of Crowds of Different Size," *Journal of Personality and Social Psychology* 13, no. 2 (1969): 79-82.

11. Robert B. Cialdini, *Influence: Science and Practice*, 5th ed. (Boston, MA: Pearson, 2008).

12. Ibid.

13. Katty Kay and Claire Shipman, "The Confidence Gap," *The Atlantic*, April 14, 2014, http://www.theatlantic.com/features/archive/2014/04/the-confidence-gap/359815/.

14. Betty Friedan, *The Feminine Mystique* (New York, NY: W.W. Norton and Co., 1963).

15. Peggy Orenstein, *Cinderella Ate My Daughter: Dispatches from the Front Lines of the New Girlie-Girl Culture* (New York, NY: Harper Paperbacks, 2012).

16. Stephanie Marcus, "Robin Thicke 'Definitely' Won't Perform With Miley Cyrus Again," *The Huffington Post*, November 10, 2013, http://www.huffingtonpost.com/2013/11/10/robin-thicke-not-perform-miley-cyrus_n_4250225.html.

17. Jess Denham, "Miley Cyrus and Britney Spears' racy music videos banned from French daytime TV," *The Independent*, January 10, 2014, http://www.independent.co.uk/arts-entertainment/music/news/miley-cyrus-and-britney-spears-racy-music-videos-banned-from-french-daytime-tv-9051743.html.

18. *Girls* [television series], 2012-present, New York, NY: Home Box Office, Inc.

19. Ibid.

20. Ibid.

21. Ibid.

22. Mark Regnerus and Jeremy Uecker, *Premarital Sex in America: How Young Americans Meet, Mate, and Think about Marrying* (New York, NY: Oxford University Press, 2011).

23. Sabrina Tavernise, "Married Couples Are No Longer a Majority, Census Finds," *The New York Times*, May 26, 2011, http://www.nytimes.com/2011/05/26/us/26marry.html.

24. Jason DeParle and Sabrina Tavernise, "For Women Under 30, Most Births Occur Outside Marriage," *The New York Times*, February 17, 2012, http://www.nytimes.com/2012/02/18/us/for-women-under-30-most-births-occur-outside-marriage.html.

25. Anjani Chandra, William D. Mosher, Casey Copen, and Catlainn Sionean, "Sexual Behavior, Sexual Attraction, and Sexual Identity in the United States: Data From the 2006-2008 National Survey of Family Growth," *National Health Statistics Report* 3, no. 36 (March 2011): 1-36.

26. Ibid.

27. Hannah Seligson, "The Orgasm Gap," *The Daily Beast*, February 9, 2009, http://www.thedailybeast.com/articles/2009/02/09/the-orgasm-gap.html.

28. Ibid.

29. Editors of Writer's Digest, *Writer's Digest University: Everything You Need to Write and Sell Your Work* (Cincinnati, OH: Writer's Digest Books, 2010).

30. "About us," Mills & Boon, http://www.millsandboon.com.au/about.

31. Joyce Lamb, "Readers' hearts remain true to romance novels," *USA Today*, February 13, 2012, http://usatoday30.usatoday.com/news/health/wellness/story/2012-02-13/Readers-hearts-remain-true-to-romance-novels/53083074/1.

32. Hanna Rosin, *The End of Men: And the Rise of Women* (New York, NY: Riverhead Hardcover, 2012).

33. "Media Influence," Rader Programs, 2013, http://www.raderprograms.com/causes-statistics/media-eating-disorders.html.

34. Edward Lovett, "Most Models Meet Criteria for Anorexia, Size 6 is Plus Size: Magazine," *ABC News*, January 12, 2012, http://abcnews.go.com/blogs/headlines/2012/01/most-models-meet-criteria-for-anorexia-size-6-is-plus-size-magazine/.

35. See note 33 above.

36. See note 34 above.

37. Daven Hiskey, "Marilyn Monroe was not even close to a size 12-16," *Today I Found Out*, April 17, 2012, http://www.todayifoundout.com/index.php/2012/04/marilyn-monroe-was-not-even-close-to-a-size-12-16/.

38. "Beauty At Any Cost," YWCA, August 2008, http://www.ywca.org/atf/cf/%7B711d5519-9e3c-4362-b753-ad138b5d352c%7D/beauty-at-any-cost.pdf.

39. "Demand for Plastic Surgery Rebounds by Almost 9%," American Society for Aesthetic Plastic Surgery, April 4, 2011, http://www.surgery.org/media/news-releases/demand-for-plastic-surgery-rebounds-by-almost-9percent.

40. Aku Ammah-Tagoe, "The Beauty Breakdown: What a Lifetime of Cosmetic Maintenance Will Cost a Modern Diva," *Newsweek*, April 20, 2010.

41. Caitlin Moran, *How to Be a Woman* (New York, NY: Harper Perennial, 2012).

42. Breeanna Hare, "'Mad Men' actress 'big'? Them's fightin' words on the Web," *CNN Entertainment*, January 21, 2010, http://www.cnn.com/2010/SHOWBIZ/01/20/globes.fashion.critiques/index.html.

43. Ariel Levy, *Female Chauvinist Pigs: Women and the Rise of Raunch Culture* (New York, NY: Free Press, 2006).

44. Deborah L. Tolman, *Dilemmas of Desire: Teenage Girls Talk about Sexuality* (Cambridge, MA: Harvard University Press, 2002).

45. Lawrence B. Finer and Jesse M. Philbin, "Sexual Initiation, Contraceptive Use, and Pregnancy Among Young Adolescents," *Pediatrics* (April 1, 2013), http://pediatrics.aappublications.org/content/early/2013/03/27/peds.2012-3495, doi:10.1542/peds.2012-3495.

46. Kaiser Family Foundation, Tina Hoff, Liberty Greene, and Julia Davis, "National Survey of Adolescents and Young Adults: Sexual Health Knowledge, Attitudes and Experiences," Henry J. Kaiser Family Foundation, http://kaiserfamilyfoundation.files.wordpress.com/2013/01/national-survey-of-adolescents-and-young-adults-sexual-health-knowledge-attitudes-and-experiences-summary-of-findings.pdf.

47. Denise D. Hallfors, Martha W. Waller, Daniel Bauer, Carol A. Ford, and Carolyn T. Halpern, "Which Comes First in Adolescence – Sex and Drugs or Depression?" *American Journal of Preventive Medicine* 29, no. 3 (2005): 163-70.

48. Lawrence B. Finer, "Trends in Premarital Sex in the United States, 1954-2003," *Public Health Rep* 122, no. 1 (2007): 73-8.

49. "Trends in the Prevalence of Sexual Behaviors and HIV Testing National YRBS: 1991-2011," Centers for Disease Control and Prevention, Youth Risk Behavior Survey, http://www.cdc.gov/healthyyouth/yrbs/pdf/us_sexual_trend_yrbs.pdf.

50. Stephanie J. Ventura, T.J. Mathews, and Brady E. Hamilton, "Births to Teenagers in the United States, 1940-2000," *National Vital Statistics Reports* 49, no. 10 (2001): 1-24.

51. Patricia Donovan, "Falling Teen Pregnancy, Birthrates: What's Behind the Declines?" *The Guttmacher Report on Public Policy* 1, no. 5 (October 1998): 6-9.

52. Heather Boonstra, "Teen Pregnancy: Trends and Lessons Learned," *The Guttmacher Report on Public Policy* 5, no. 1 (February 2002): 7-10.

53. NPR Staff, "Teen Pregnancy Declines, But U.S. Still Lags," *NPR*, August 19, 2012, http://www.npr.org/2012/08/19/159252419/teen-pregnancy-declines-but-u-s-still-lags-behind.

54. Esther Perel, *Mating in Captivity: Unlocking Erotic Intelligence* (New York, NY: Harper Perennial, 2007).

55. Peter S. Karofsky, Lan Zeng, and Michael R. Kosorok, "Relationship between adolescent-parental communication and initiation of first intercourse by adolescents," *Journal of Adolescent Health* 28, no. 1 (2001): 41-5.

56. Douglas Kirby and Gina Lepore, "Sexual Risk and Protective Factors: Factors Affecting Teen Sexual Behavior, Pregnancy, Childbearing and Sexually Transmitted Disease," ETR Associates and The National Campaign to Prevent Teen and Unplanned Pregnancy, November 26, 2007, http://recapp.etr.org/recapp/documents/theories/RiskProtectiveFactors200712.pdf.

57. See note 43 above.

58. E. L. James, *Fifty Shades of Grey* (New York, NY: Vintage, 2012).

59. Ibid.

60. James J. Heckman and Paul A. LaFontaine, "The American High School Graduation Rate: Trends and Levels," *Review of Economics and Statistics* 92, no. 2 (2010): 244-62.

61. Terris Ross, Grace Kena, Amy Rathbun, Angelina KewalRamani, Jijun Zhang, Paul Kristapovich, and Eileen Manning, "Higher Education: Gaps in Access and Persistence Study," *U.S. Department of Education*, August 2012, http://nces.ed.gov/pubs2012/2012046.pdf.

62. See note 32 above.

63. Anne-Marie Slaughter, "Why Women Still Can't Have It All," *The Atlantic*, June 13, 2012, http://www.theatlantic.com/magazine/archive/2012/07/why-women-still-cant-have-it-all/309020/.

64. Michele J. Gelfand and Anu Realo, "Individualism-Collectivism and Accountability in Intergroup Negotiations," *Journal of Applied Psychology* 84, no. 5 (1999): 721-36.

3

65. *Bridget Jones's Diary* [motion picture], Miramax Films, Universal Pictures, StudioCanal, Working Title Films, and Little Bird, 2001.

66. Barry Schwartz, *The Paradox of Choice: Why More Is Less* (New York, NY: Harper Perennial, 2005).

67. Ibid.

68. Susan A. Patton, letter to the editor, *The Daily Princetonian*, March 29, 2013, http://dailyprincetonian.com/opinion/2013/03/letter-to-the-editor-advice-for-the-young-women-of-princeton-the-daughters-i-never-had/.

69. Julia Shaw, "Marry Young: I Got Married at 23. What Are the Rest of You Waiting For?" *Slate*, April 1, 2013, http://www.slate.com/articles/double_x/doublex/2013/04/i_married_young_what_are_the_rest_of_you_waiting_for.html.

70. "The Wage Gap is Stagnant in Last Decade," National Women's Law Center, Fact Sheet, September, 2012, http://www.nwlc.org/sites/default/files/pdfs/poverty_day_wage_gap_sheet.pdf.

71. James Surowiecki, *The Wisdom of Crowds* (New York, NY: Random House, 2005).

72. Ibid.

73. Frédérique R. E. Smink, Daphne van Hoeken, and Hans W. Hoek, "Epidemiology of Eating Disorders: Incidence, Prevalence and Mortality Rates," *Current Psychiatry Reports* 14, no. 4 (2012): 406-14, http://www.ncbi.nlm.nih.gov/pubmed/22644309.

74. "Cosmetic Surgery National Data Bank Statistics 2012," The American Society for Anesthetic Plastic Surgery, 2012, http://www.surgery.org/sites/default/files/ASAPS-2012-Stats.pdf.

75. "Sexualization of Girls: Executive Summary," American Psychological Association, 2007, http://www.apa.org/pi/women/programs/girls/report.aspx.

76. "End the Sexualization of Girls and Young Women in Mainstream Media," The Advocates for Human Rights, hand-out, http://www.theadvocatesforhumanrights.org/uploads/killing_us_softly_4_handout_online_challenge_the_media_handout_for_film.pdf.

77. Noam Shpancer, "If Only...Gender Differences in Sexual Regret," *Psychology Today*, June 4, 2013, http://www.psychologytoday.com/blog/insight-therapy/201306/if-only-gender-differences-in-sexual-regret.

78. See note 65 above.

79. Shiri Cohen, Marc S. Schulz, Emily Weiss, and Robert J. Waldinger, "Eye of the Beholder: The Individual and Dyadic Contributions of Empathic Accuracy and Perceived Empathic Effort to Relationship Satisfaction," *Journal of Family Psychology* 26, no. 2 (2012): 236-45.

80. Elizabeth Svoboda, "Field Guide to the People-Pleaser: May I Serve As Your Doormat?" *Psychology Today*, May 1, 2008, http://www.psychologytoday.com/articles/200805/field-guide-the-people-pleaser-may-i-serve-your-doormat.

4

81. David A. Puts, "Beauty and the beast: mechanisms of sexual selection in humans," *Evolution and Human Behavior* 31 (2010): 157-75.

82. Gregory L. Jantz, "Brain Differences Between Genders," *Psychology Today*, February 27, 2014, http://www.psychologytoday.com/blog/hope-relationships/201402/brain-differences-between-genders.

83. David Buller, *Adapting Minds: Evolutionary Psychology and the Persistent Quest for Human Nature* (Cambridge, MA: Bradford Books, 2006).

84. Ibid.

85. Sheryl Walters, "Regular Sex Improves Health and Doubles Life Expectancy," Naturalnews.com, January 22, 2009, http://www.naturalnews.com/025393_health_WHO_life.html#.

86. Lawrence K. Altman, "More Orgasms, More Years of Life?" *The New York Times*, December 23, 1997, http://www.nytimes.com/1997/12/23/science/more-orgasms-more-years-of-life.html.

87. Dan Slater, "Darwin Was Wrong About Dating," *The New York Times*, January 12, 2013, http://www.nytimes.com/2013/01/13/opinion/sunday/darwin-was-wrong-about-dating.html.

88. Deborah Tannen, *You Just Don't Understand: Women and Men in Conversation* (New York, NY: William Morrow Paperbacks, 2007).

89. John Gray, *Men Are From Mars, Women Are From Venus: A Practical Guide for Improving Communication and Getting What You Want in Your Relationships* (New York, NY: HarperCollins Publishers, 1992).

90. Deborah Cameron, *The Myth of Mars and Venus: Do Men and Women Really Speak Different Languages?* (Oxford, UK: Oxford University Press, 2009).

91. Ibid.

92. Ibid.

93. Louann Brizendine, *The Female Brain* (New York, NY: Harmony Books, 2007).

94. Louann Brizendine, *The Male Brain* (New York, NY: Harmony Books, 2011).

95. Emily Bazelon, "A Mind of His Own," *The New York Times: Sunday Book Review*, March 25, 2010, http://www.nytimes.com/2010/03/28/books/review/Bazelon-t.html.

96. Louann Brizendine, "Powerful Women in Love: Modern Male Brains and the Young, Powerful Women Who Love Them," *The Huffington Post*, posted June 7, 2010, updated November 17, 2011, http://www.huffingtonpost.com/louann-brizendine/relationship-love-modern_b_599720.html.

97. Lise Eliot, *Pink Brain, Blue Brain: How Small Differences Grow Into Troublesome Gaps – And What We Can Do About It* (New York, NY: Mariner Books, 2010).

98. Ibid.

99. Ibid.

100. "Pink Brain, Blue Brain," Lise Eliot, the website of Lise Eliot, http://www.liseeliot.com/pink-brain-blue-brain.

101. B. A. Arnow, L. Millheiser, A. Garrett, M. Lake Polan, G. H. Glover, K. R. Hill, A. Lightbody, C. Watson, L. Banner, T. Smart, T. Buchanan, and J.E. Desmond, "Women with hypoactive sexual desire disorder compared to normal females: A functional magnetic resonance imaging study," *Neuroscience* 158, no. 2 (January 23, 2009): 484-502.

102. Uwe Hartmann, Susanne Philippsohn, Kristina Heiser, and Claudia Ruffer-Hesse, "Low sexual desire in midlife and older women: personality factors, psychosocial development, present sexuality," *Menopause* 11, no. 6 (November/December 2004): 726-40.

103. Christopher Ryan, "Why There Will Never Be Viagra for Women," *Psychology Today*, June 25, 2010, http://www.psychologytoday.com/blog/sex-dawn/201006/why-there-will-never-be-viagra-women.

104. "Sexual Desire – The Real Female Orgasm," Oprah.com, August 14, 2009, http://www.oprah.com/relationships/Sexual-Desire-The-Real-Female-Orgasm.

105. Roy F. Baumeister, "The Reality of the Male Sex Drive," *Psychology Today*, December 8, 2010, http://www.psychologytoday.com/blog/cultural-animal/201012/the-reality-the-male-sex-drive.

106. Dietrich Klusmann, "Sexual Motivation and the Duration of Partnership," *Archives of Sexual Behavior* 31, no. 3 (June 2002): 275-87.

107. Leon F. Seltzer, "The Triggers of Sexual Desire Part 2: What's Erotic for Women?" *Psychology Today,* May 14, 2012, http://www.psychologytoday.com/blog/evolution-the-self/201205/the-triggers-sexual-desire-part-2-whats-erotic-women.

108. Daniel Bergner, "What Do Women Want?" *The New York Times,* January 22, 2009, http://www.nytimes.com/2009/01/25/magazine/25desire-t.html.

109. Marta Meana, personal communication, September 2, 2014.

110. Neal J. Roese, Ginger L. Pennington, Jill Coleman, Maria Janicki, Norman P. Li, and Douglas T. Kenrick, "Sex Differences in Regret: All For Love or Some For Lust?" *Personality and Social Psychology Bulletin* 32, no. 6 (June 2006): 770-80.

111. "Study Examines Potential Evolutionary Role of 'Sexual Regret' in Human Survival and Reproduction," The University of Texas at Austin, http://www.utexas.edu/news/2013/11/25/human-survival-and-reproduction/.

112. See note 93 above.

113. Carlene Bauer, "This is your brain in love," Salon.com, http://www.salon.com/2004/01/27/fisher_6/.

114. Helen Fisher, *Why We Love: The Nature and Chemistry of Romantic Love* (New York, NY: Holt Paperbacks, 2004).

115. Anita H. Clayton, Helen E. Fisher, Philip R. Muskin, and Serena Yuan Volpp, "Sex, Sexuality, and Serotonin: Do Sexual Side Effects of Most Antidepressants Jeopardize Romantic Love and Marriage?" CME activity, originally presented by Helen E. Fisher, Medscape, http://www.medscape.org/viewarticle/482059.

116. Linda Dyett, "Should Women Consider Taking Testosterone?" *The Huffington Post,* July 30, 2013, http://www.huffingtonpost.com/2013/07/30/testosterone-women-hormone-therapy_n_3634847.html.

117. "Changes in Hormone Levels," The North American Menopause Society, 2014, http://www.menopause.org/for-women/sexual-health-menopause-online/changes-at-midlife/changes-in-hormone-levels.

118. Daniel Goleman, "Aggression in Men: Hormone Levels Are a Key," *The New York Times,* July 17, 1990, http://www.nytimes.com/1990/07/17/science/aggression-in-men-hormone-levels-are-a-key.html.

119. See note 93 above.

120. Terri D. Conley, Amy C. Moors, Jes L. Matsick, Ali Ziegler, and Brandon A. Valentine, "Women, Men, and the Bedroom: Methodological and Conceptual Insights That Narrow, Reframe, and Eliminate Gender Differences in Sexuality," *Current Directions in Psychological Science* 20, no. 5 (October 2011): 296-300, doi:10.1177/0963721411418467.

121. Barbara Pease and Alan Pease, *Why Men Want Sex and Women Need Love: Solving the Mystery of Attraction* (New York, NY: Harmony, 2010).

122. Ibid.

123. See note 107 above.

124. Leon F. Seltzer, "The Triggers of Sexual Desire: Men vs. Women," *Psychology Today*, May 11, 2012, http://www.psychologytoday.com/blog/evolution-the-self/201205/the-triggers-sexual-desire-men-vs-women.

125. See note 114 above.

126. Roger Dobson, "Love on the brain," *The Independent*, October 4, 2010, http://www.independent.co.uk/news/science/love-on-the-brain-2096672.html.

127. See note 115 above.

128. Ibid.

129. See note 114 above.

130. James R. Roney, Zachary L. Simmons, "Hormonal predictors of sexual motivation in natural menstrual cycles," *Hormones and Behavior* 63, no. 4 (April 2013): 636-45, doi:10.1016/j.yhbeh.2013.02.013.

131. Margaret M. McCarthy, "Estrogen modulation of oxytocin and its relation to behavior," *Advances in Experimental Medicine and Biology* 395 (February 1995): 235-45.

132. See note 117 above.

133. Donatella Marazziti, Bernardo Dell'Osso, Stefano Baroni, Francesco Mungai, Mario Catena, Paola Rucci, Francesco Albanese, Gino Giannaccini, Laura Betti, Laura Fabbrini, Paola Italiani, Alessandro Del Debbio, Antonio Lucacchini, and Liliana Dell'Osso, "A relationship between oxytocin and anxiety of romantic attachment," *Clinical Practice and Epidemiology in Mental Health* 2, no. 28 (October 11, 2006): 1-6, doi:10.1186/1745-0179-2-28.

134. R. R. Thompson, K. George, J. C. Walton, S. P. Orr, and J. Benson, "Sex-specific influences of vasopressin on human social communication," *Proceedings of the National Academy of Sciences of the United States of America* 103, no. 20 (May 2006): 7889-94, doi:10.1073/pnas.0600406103.

135. D. P. Benziger and J. Edelson, "Absorption from the vagina," *Drug Metabolism Reviews* 14, no. 2 (February 1983): 137-68, doi:10.3109/03602538308991387.

136. Philip G. Ney, "The Intravaginal Absorption of Male Generated Hormones and Their Possible Effect on Female Behavior," *Medical Hypotheses* 20, no. 2 (June 1986): 221-31, doi:10.1016/0306-9877(86)90128-3.

137. Gordon G. Gallup, Rebecca L. Burch, and Steven M. Platek, "Does Semen have antidepressant properties?" *Archives of Sexual Behavior* 31, no. 3 (July 2002): 289-93, doi:10.1023/A:1015257004839.

138. "'Love Hormone' Promotes Bonding," Debra Kain, UC San Diego, News Center, http://ucsdnews.ucsd.edu/archive/newsrel/health/02-08LoveHormone.asp.

139. Michael Miller, "Sad Brain, Happy Brain," *Newsweek*, September 12, 2008, http://www.newsweek.com/sad-brain-happy-brain-88455.

140. See note 58 above.

141. Shiri Cohen, Marc S. Schulz, Emily Weiss, and Robert J. Waldinger, "Eye of the Beholder: The Individual and Dyadic Contributions of Empathic Accuracy and Perceived Empathic Effort to Relationship Satisfaction," *Journal of Family Psychology* 26, no. 2 (2012): 236-45, doi:10.1037/a0027488.

142. Ibid.

143. David Schnarch, *Passionate Marriage: Keeping Love and Intimacy Alive in Committed Relationships* (New York, NY: W.W. Norton & Company, 2009). [Emphasis in original.]

144. Ibid.

145. Ibid. [Emphasis in original.]

146. Lauren Slater, "Monkey love," *The Boston Globe*, March 21, 2004, http://www.boston.com/news/globe/ideas/articles/2004/03/21/monkey_love/.

147. Thomas Lewis, Fari Amini, and Richard Lannon, *A General Theory of Love* (New York, NY: Vintage, 2001).

148. Ibid.

5

149. *Sex and the City* [television series], 1998-2004, New York, NY: Home Box Office, Inc.

150. Greg Behrendt and Liz Tuccillo, *He's Just Not That Into You: The No-Excuses Truth to Understanding Guys* (New York, NY: Gallery Books, 2009).

151. Ellen Fein and Sherrie Schneider, *The Rules: Time-Tested Secrets for Capturing the Heart of Mr. Right* (New York, NY: Grand Central Publishing, 1995).

152. See note 11 above.

153. Lauren Duca, "'Bachelor' and 'Bachelorette' Couples' Success in Infographics," *The Huffington Post*, August 9, 2013, http://www.huffingtonpost.com/2013/08/12/bachelor-couples_n_3728241.html.

154. Lauren Said-Moorhouse, "5 reasons why we love Gloria Steinem," *CNN*, March 25, 2014, http://www.cnn.com/2014/03/25/living/5-reasons-why-we-love-gloria-steinem/.

155. See note 18 above.

156. Ibid.

157. Ibid.

158. Alanna Vagianos, "21 Ways Gloria Steinem Taught Us To Be Better Women," *The Huffington Post*, March 25, 2014, http://www.huffingtonpost.com/2014/03/25/ways-gloria-steinem-taught-us-to-be-better-women_n_5022031.html.

159. Jennifer Frey, "Jane Austen: A Love Story. For England's 228-Year-Old Novelist, the Ink Has Yet to Dry," *The Washington Post Magazine*, August 22, 2004: D1 & D6.

6

160. Carol Dweck, *Mindset: The New Psychology of Success* (New York, NY: Random House Publishing Group, 2007).

161. "Understanding forgiveness," PBS, *This Emotional Life*, 2011, http://www.pbs.org/thisemotionallife/topic/forgiveness/understanding-forgiveness.

162. Nora Ephron, 1996 Wellesley commencement address, Wellesley College, http://www.wellesley.edu/events/commencement/archives/1996commencement.

163. See note 80 above.

7

164. *When Harry Met Sally* [motion picture], Castle Rock Entertainment and Nelson Entertainment, 1989.

165. Jane Austen, *Pride and Prejudice* (New York, NY: C. Scribner's Sons, 1918).

8

166. Agnes de Mille, *Dance to the Piper* (London, UK: Columbus Books, 1987), 94.

9

167. "Statistics," National Institute of Mental Health, http://www.nimh. nih.gov/Statistics/index.shtml.

10

168. Malcolm Gladwell, *The Tipping Point: How Little Things Can Make a Big Difference* (New York, NY: Back Bay Books, 2002).

169. Ibid.

170. Ibid.

171. "'I' Statements not 'You' Statements," Conflict Research Consortium, University of Colorado, 1998, http://www.colorado.edu/conflict/peace/treatment/istate.htm.

172. John Gottman, *Why Marriages Succeed or Fail: And How You Can Make Yours Last* (New York, NY: Simon & Schuster, 1995).

173. See note 171 above.

174. Liz Szabo, "Puberty too soon: Girls are maturing faster than ever, and doctors are not sure why." *USA Today*, April, 11, 2011, http://usatoday30. usatoday.com/printedition/news/20110411/1apuberty11_cv.art.htm.

175. See note 154 above.

176. Gloria Steinem, *Outrageous Acts and Everyday Rebellions*, 2nd ed. (New York, NY: Holt Paperbacks, 1995). [Emphasis in original.]

177. Emily Bennington, "The World Will Be Saved By the Western Woman," *The Huffington Post*, December 11, 2012, http://www. huffingtonpost.com/emily-bennington/western-women_b_2277916.html.

178. Loren Toussaint and Jon R. Webb, "Gender Differences in the Relationship Between Empathy and Forgiveness," *The Journal of Social Psychology* 145, no. 6 (December 2005): 673-85, doi:10.3200/SOCP.145.6.673-686.

179. Rhawn Joseph, "Competition Between Women," *Psychology* 22, (1985): 1-11.

180. See note 176 above. [Emphasis in original.]

181. Cheryl Brown Travis, *Women and Health Psychology: Mental Health Issues* (New York, NY: Psychology Press, 2014).

182. "Self-Help Groups: Are They Effective?" Wichita State University, Center for Community Support and Research, 2014, http://webs.wichita. edu/depttools/depttoolsmemberfiles/ccsr/Self%20Help%20Group%20 Articles/Self-Help%20Groups.%20Are%20They%20Effective.pdf.

183. Erica Jong, "Is Sex Passé?" *The New York Times*, July 9, 2011, http:// www.nytimes.com/2011/07/10/opinion/sunday/10sex.html?_r=0.

Appendix A:
Related Books and Articles

1

Baird, Julia. "Mad Women, Not Mad Men. On TV, the seeds of a revolution." *Newsweek*, August 23 & 30, 2010, 26.

"Campus Confidential: Everything she wanted to know about campus coupling—and wasn't afraid to ask." *Stanford Magazine*, March/April 2008. http://alumni.stanford.edu/get/page/magazine/article/?article_id=31491.

Kantrowitz, Barbara. "How Women Lead." *Newsweek*, October 24, 2005, 46-8.

Miller, Lisa. "Sexual Revolution Part II: The fight over abstinence at Harvard." *Newsweek*, November 16, 2009, 26.

Rosenwaike, Polly. "'In Praise of Messy Lives,' by Katie Roiphe." *San Francisco Chronicle*, September 7, 2012, updated September 10, 2012. http://www.sfchronicle.com/books/article/In-Praise-of-Messy-Lives-by-Katie-Roiphe-3848838.php.

Toepfer, Susan. "Gloria Steinem Looks Back—and Forward." *More*, August 12, 2011. http://www.more.com/gloria-steinem-hbo-documentary.

2

Bolick, Kate. "All the Single Ladies." *The Atlantic*, September 30, 2011. http://www.theatlantic.com/magazine/archive/2011/11/all-the-single-ladies/308654/.

Coontz, Stephanie. *Marriage, a History: How Love Conquered Marriage.* New York, NY: Penguin Books, 2006.

———. *A Strange Stirring: The Feminine Mystique and American Women at the Dawn of the 1960s.* New York, NY: Basic Books, 2012.

Holmes, Anna. "The Disposable Woman." *The New York Times,* March 3, 2011. http://www.nytimes.com/2011/03/04/opinion/04holmes.html.

Murray, Sara. "Women More Likely Than Men to Graduate College at 22." *The Wall Street Journal,* January 29, 2010. http://blogs.wsj.com/economics/2010/01/29/women-more-likely-than-men-to-graduate-college-at-22/.

Simmons, Rachel. *The Curse of the Good Girl: Raising Authentic Girls with Courage and Confidence.* New York, NY: Penguin Books, 2010.

Stewart, Carrie. "What's Your Sexting Plan?" *Marie Claire,* July 1, 2013. http://www.marieclaire.com/sex-love/whats-your-sexting-plan-sending-photos-of-penis.

"Study points out risks of nonromantic sexual relationships." University of Iowa News Service. April 1, 2010. http://news-releases.uiowa.edu/2010/april/040110study-relationships.html.

Williams, Alex. "The End of Courtship?" *The New York Times,* January 11, 2013. http://www.nytimes.com/2013/01/13/fashion/the-end-of-courtship.html.

3

Haddock, Vicki. "The Happiness Quotient." *San Francisco Chronicle Magazine,* December 30, 2007, 19-27.

Hinshaw, Stephen. *The Triple Bind: Saving Our Teenage Girls from Today's Pressures.* With Rachel Kranz. New York, NY: Random House/Ballantine, 2009.

Taylor, Kate. "Sex on Campus: She Can Play That Game, Too." *The New York Times,* July 14, 2013, 1-7.

4

Buller, David J. *Adapting Minds: Evolutionary Psychology and the Persistent Quest for Human Nature.* Cambridge, MA: Bradford Books, 2006.

Buss, David. *Evolutionary Psychology: The New Science of the Mind.* 2nd ed. Boston, MA: Allyn & Bacon, 2003.

Fisher, Helen. *Why We Love: The Nature and Chemistry of Romantic Love.* New York, NY: Holt Paperbacks, 2004.

6

Estés, Clarissa Pinkola. *Women Who Run with the Wolves*. New York, NY: Ballantine Books, 1996.

Kross, Ethan and Ozlem Ayduk. "Making Meaning out of Negative Experiences by Self-Distracting." *Current Directions in Psychological Science* 20, no. 3 (June 2011): 187-91.

Milne, David. "People Can Learn Markers On Road to Resilience." *Psychiatric News*, January 19, 2007. http://psychnews.psychiatryonline.org/newsArticle.aspx?articleid=110644.

"Proof Love at First Sight Exists." *BBC News*, Sept. 10, 2004. http://news.bbc.co.uk/2/hi/health/3643822.stm.

7

Goldberg, Herb. *The Hazards of Being Male: Surviving the Myth of Masculine Privilege*. New York, NY: Nash Publishing, 1976.

9

Estes, Clarissa Pinkola. *Women Who Run with the Wolves*. New York, NY: Ballantine Books, 1996.

Kelly, Jennifer. "Stigma Proves Hard to Eradicate Despite Multiple Advances." *Psychiatric News*, January 7, 2011. http://www.psychiatryonline.org/newsArticle.aspx?articleid=113964.

Kirwan-Taylor, Helen. "Are you an HSP?" *Marie Claire*, December 2010, 224-28.

Marano, Hara Estroff. "Oh, Brother!" *Psychology Today*, July 1, 2010. http://www.psychologytoday.com/articles/201006/oh-brother.

Walsh, Kate, Carla Kmett Danielson, Jenna L. McCauley, Benjamin E. Saunders, Dean G. Kilpatrick, and Heidi S. Resnick. "National Prevalence of Posttraumatic Stress Disorder Among Sexually Revictimized Adolescent, College, and Adult Household-Residing Women." *Archives of General Psychiatry* 69, no. 9 (2012): 935-42. doi:10.1001/archgenpsychiatry.2012.132.

10

Bennett, Jessica. "The Beauty Advantage." *Newsweek*. Filed July 19, 2010, updated July 29, 2011. http://www.newsweek.com/beauty-advantage-how-looks-affect-your-work-your-career-your-life-74313.

Jong, Erica. *What Do Women Want?: Essays by Erica Jong*. New York, NY: Tarcher, 2007.

Seligman, Katherine. "Pursuing happiness in perilous times." *San Francisco Chronicle*, November 16, 2008: F1, F5.

Steinem, Gloria. *Outrageous Acts and Everyday Rebellions*, 2nd ed. New York, NY: Holt Paperbacks, 1995.

Wallis, Jim. "Good News About a Bad Economy." *AARP Bulletin*, March 2010: 38.

Index

D